ROOM COLOUR

FOR YOUR HOME

An Informative and Workable Guide to Learning, Choosing and Working with Colour in Your Home

By
Belinda Corani
of Home Conscious Interior Design

Published by
Home Conscious Ltd

http://www.homeconscious.com

ISBN: 978-0-9956921-0-7

DEDICATION

This ebook is dedicated to my mother, whose love of nature and the colours that are found within it continue to inspire me. For everything you have taught me, thank you.

WORKING WITH COLOUR IN INTERIOR DESIGN

Why This Book Was Written:

You've probably found me through either my website or my podcast – or maybe through a recommendation. I'm happy to say I have had many recommendations over the years. But either way, I'm happy you found me.

I've been working in Interior Design for many years. Over those years, I've been asked many questions and have seen many properties. One of the first questions clients ask me (after "do you think it needs much work?") is "What colours do you think I should go for?"

It stands to reason that most people aren't interested in plumbing and drainage, or even curtain poles for that matter. But EVERYONE gets involved with colour. Husbands and wives have deep discussions, children demand a say on what colours go where and who gets to have them in their bedroom. And if you are an interior designer, and your clients have extended family and friends, they'll all want a say too.

So, this guide is for anyone that wants to think for themselves. Someone who wants to weigh up the colours and perhaps be introduced to some new ones. It's a handy guide for the variants of colours with some tip top advice on things to consider and look out for.

Things to note:

- This ebook is a guide, and the purpose of this guide is to do just that – guide you.
- It's not set in concrete (sorry, industry joke) and it's just my opinion (and rather a lot of others too..). Please take this Ebook as you would any other professional, teaching you what they know. Everyone has different opinions and experience on interiors and you, (or your friends!), won't always agree with my recommendations.
- I am here to help you – so if you would like this updated, or any further information, or would just like me to do another book on another subject – just let me know.

CONTACTING ME

If you have any questions and would like an honest opinion on something at your home or property – please get in touch through my Facebook Group or if you just want to follow along, head over to my Facebook Page. You can always find me on Twitter of course which may be a bit faster!

Here are some place to find me..

www.homeconscious.com

TABLE OF CONTENTS

DEDICATION 3

WORKING WITH COLOUR IN INTERIOR DESIGN 5

CONTACTING ME 7

WHAT CAN COLOUR DO FOR YOU? 13

    Pink 24

    Pale Pink 25

    Cerise Pink 26

    Dusky Pink 27

    Blue 28

    Ice Blue 29

    Turquoise 30

    Airforce Blue 31

    Navy 32

    Aqua 33

    Peacock Blue 34

    Dusty Blue 35

    Powder Blue 36

    Red 37

    Red 38

    Crimson 39

    Burgundy 40

    Maroon 41

    Yellow 42

    Golden Yellow 43

    Lemon 44

    Primrose 45

ROOM COLOUR

Brown 47
Tan 48
Beige, Taupe, Fawn… 49
…and Cream 50
Orange 51
Terracotta 52
Burnt Orange 53
Green 54
Pea Green 55
Garden Green 56
Grass Green 57
Dusky Green 58
Teal Green 59
Lime Green 60
Olive Green 61
Purple 62
Lilac 63
Plum 64
Purple 65
Lavender 66
Damson 67
Grey 68
Lead/Dark Grey 69
Gunmetal 70
Pale Grey/French Grey 71
White 72

MAKING A SCHEME FLOW 73

YOUR PROJECT – YOUR SCHEME 76

STEP 1: WHAT WILL YOU USE THE ROOM FOR? 78

STEP 2: WHAT COLOUR BASE ARE YOU THINKING OF USING? 80

STEP 3: WORKING WITH DAYLIGHT AND COLOUR - WHICH DIRECTION IS YOUR ROOM FACING? 82

STEP 4: DO YOU HAVE AN EXACT SHADE OR TINT IN MIND? 85

STEP 5: FEATURES, HIGHLIGHTS, ISSUES, PROPORTIONS 86

STEP 6: WOODWORK CHOICES 91

STEP 7: ASSESSING YOUR FURNITURE AND ACCESSORIES 98

STEP 8: CHOOSING SPECIFIC SHADES 100

THANK YOU 107

ABOUT THE AUTHOR 109

DISCLAIMER 111

PHOTO CREDITS: 113

WHAT CAN COLOUR DO FOR YOU?

Colour plays an important part in our mood and sometimes how we perceive our life and our surroundings. In this guide I will take you through the various different colours with photographs showing you how these colours can be used. I want to show you, through colour, how to make your home reflective of your style and character. I will also teach you what colour combinations to avoid and what combinations to use using your favourite shades and tones.

Proven things that colour provides

- Create visual feast for your eyes
- Provides cool or warm tones for a room
- Lifts mood and spirit by the use of discernible colour

Using Colour – The Fear

For too long interiors have been very neutral and people have become frightened of colour. They've especially become frightened of how their interiors will be perceived by others. Particularly family or friends. I find that they start with bold intentions and then in the face of opposition and doubt, they fold, and head over to a neutral palette.

When I first started my interior design journey, I could never understand how everyone seemed to be obsessed with painting their walls in a neutral colour and then seemed unhappy with the result. They called their finished scheme bland, flat and boring. So, why did they choose that cream colour for the walls? Or mushroom? Or taupe? Or grey? It became apparent that most people were, in effect, not brave; but were following advice given by somebody else. Furthermore, this 'neutral advice' was compounded by the equally usual practice of lifting their chosen colour scheme from the pages of a magazine. 'It worked in someone else's property' they ask, 'why didn't it in mine?' The answer is usually five-fold:

ROOM COLOUR

1. the photo has been 'Photoshopped' or re-touched and enhanced so you don't get a true representation
2. the lighting is not remotely similar – your friend's room might be south facing, yours might be north facing. This is going to change things dramatically
3. the room proportions or even the size of room are going to impact the colour
4. the furniture and accessories that are in your room are changing the colour of your walls when your eye falls on them
5. your decorator has not executed the job well, leaving gaps or transparent parts on the wall (this is an unlikely reason, but it has happened!)

Any of those five reasons may be the answer as to why the scheme didn't work for them. But the real issue is that they're not being brave and going for what they really want. It might help to have a basic knowledge of colour and have a good overview of what colours there are and how they relate to each other.

The Colour Wheel

Much has been written about the colour wheel and much of it confusing and contradictory. Most designers learn about the colour wheel early on in their careers, and it is a useful to know, when you are at the start and exploring the rudiments of colour. But it is not something that you will use on a daily basis. I'm mentioning it here as I want to dispel the myth that you have to live your life by it.

It's useful for two things. Firstly, when you're learning, you can see what colours are opposite of each other; so, Red and Green, Blue and Orange etc. Secondly, this knowledge can be used as a pointer when you are thinking up some interesting colour schemes.

So, you might have a Purple sofa (yours or a clients) to work around, but would like to add some kind of colour to the walls. If you think of the colour wheel and what goes with Purple, one place that you could start with would be Yellow, that being the opposite of Purple. So, it could be that you look at a Pale Lemon as one of the choices you look at. Maybe another option would be a Lime Green, as Green is next to Yellow on the wheel. The colour wheel just gives you a few pointers and a sure place to start. Other, more detailed colour wheels, are often broken down further into 'hues' of the same base colour. This can get confusing and overwhelming. The trick is not to get too tied to it. The wheel does give you the opposite colours of the main colours but it is not exhaustive – you will play around with shades and tones as they come to you and as you gain experience.

Understanding Undertones

When looking at any color, your eyes can quickly identify the basic colour. This is so that when you see it you say "oh, that's blue." The undertone is the subtle influence of one colour underneath the bass colour, and it's this that distinguishes it from another colour. The undertone is not always obvious until it is paired with other colours, or appears under certain lighting though!

How Can You Identify an Undertone?

If you are trying to find the undertone for a blue, then compare it next to a true blue. Does it look more green next to the 'true blue'? This will give you an idea of whether your blue has more yellow or green undertone. It's not always easy to find a true colour for comparison, so use a colour wheel to be sure you have the purest colour for comparison.

Sampling a paint colour in your home is the best way to check a colour if you're still not sure about what undertone you're looking at. Everything from floor and worktop surfaces to lighting, and even plants outside, can bring out surprising undertones on your painted walls. For example, as stated earlier, light bulbs can be warm, cool, or natural, and can affect, or bring out the undertones at once.

Which Undertones cause problems?

Pink and green are the most difficult to work with. Even the most neutral grey or beige can appear green in certain settings. Green undertones aren't always easily visible until they are set next to your joinery or flooring with its own undertones of yellow or orange. This is what makes the green undertones problematic. The prevalence of warm woods in our homes really sets off even the slightest green undertone.

Pink is another issue, especially with taupe, sand, fawn and beige. All it takes is a slight prevalence of red in the neutral, for pink to emerge.

Now, I happen to like that deep terracotta pink but if you don't then it's worth looking at beiges and taupes carefully to see that they are totally right for your property. Try them in different lights at different times of the day.

How to manage undertones...

If you can see that the colours you've chosen have an undertone that doesn't work in the room, then try warmer or cooler hues until it looks right. Or look at different colours altogether. Make sure you have the furniture and especially the lighting in place as these will make all the difference. USE YOUR EYES! Don't be sidetracked by jargon - trust your eyesight.

Explaining Colour Terms

Whilst we're talking about undertones, we may as well explain some jargon and clear up a few inaccuracies surrounding colour terms..

Chroma

Chroma is the Greek word for colour. Chroma describes the saturation of any particular colour. You don't need to worry about this when you are choosing colour for your walls at home as the description is generally used by manufacturers creating colours for their companies and businesses.

Tints and Shades:

Tints and shades describe whether a particular colour is either light (a tint) or dark (a shade). So this literally denotes a colour that has been lightened by adding white or darkened by adding black. A clever way to remember this is to remember that shade <u>darkens</u> the ground on a sunny day - ie shades are darker, therefore tints are lighter.

A **Tone** is a colour that has both black AND white added to it in the form of Grey. Most of the 'dusky' colours fall under 'tone'.

Hues

A hue is something slightly different in that it pertains to the colour wheel. You don't need to look at a colour wheel in order to choose the paint for your walls but it is worth remembering that all of the colours in the colour wheel can be broken up into different hues use of the same colour. A hue is more a way of saying that something is still 'orange'. For example, it's just a little lighter or darker or greyer..it's still a hue of orange.

Cusp Colour

Cusp Colour is a relatively new term describing colours that appear to change under different lighting conditions. Different light bulbs (or 'lamps' as we call them in the trade) throw off different warmths, and it is these cusp colours (mostly blues and purples) that change the most. Again, this is not something that you should worry about until you choose your light bulbs for your light fittings. It certainly shouldn't dictate what colour you want to use in your home.

RAL

RAL Is a German abbreviation that stands for a colour matching system, originating in Germany during 1927. RAL is used for painting and finishing colours in construction, architecture and even road signage. Each colour in the RAL collection has a four digit number so that it can be accurately identified. Each colour also has a name, but these vary from country to country so it is best to work with the 4 digit number rather than names, if you are using the RAL system. Today the RAL system includes over 1800 colours.

Pantone

Pantone is another colour matching system and this originated from 1950s America. Well known for using the four main ink printing colours of cyan, magenta, yellow and black to create its shades, Pantone today is just as well known for its yearly declaration of the 'Colour Of The Year'. 2016 is currently a mauve/blue shade called Serenity! These annual colours are chosen by various colour representatives from around the world and they reflect what is trending, popular and what has caught the zeitgeist of the general public's mood. Trending is big business and colour is one of the key indicators of where society is going and what it's feeling.

So, let's get started with planning a colour scheme...

HOW MANY COLOURS SHOULD I USE IN A SCHEME?

This is one of the most common questions that I get asked. There is a general rule of 3-4 colours to be used in any scheme. This is regularly flouted! However, the premise of 3-4 colours in a room is a good way to keep the room co-ordinated and controlled. It also gives you some boundaries to work with. There are thousands of colours and just as many combinations to create with those shades. It's important that you have some limitations so ensure that you're not overwhelmed and can move forward with your project. The biggest thing to bear in mind is that when you start adding the little things (books, ornaments, table lamps, photographs frames), these will bring extra colour and texture to your scheme, so it will not look flat.

If we look at the 4 colour scheme:

Colour 1 – this is the main colour that the room shows – (note, this can be a neutral too if your scheme is all neutrals)

Colour 2 – this is the secondary colour in your scheme – (very noticeable but not the main colour)

Colour 3 – this is just a small amount limited to one large item or a few small items

Neutral 1 – this is your base neutral. Either Warm (example Beiges and Creams) or Cool (example Greys and Whites).

There is one other option to add to this list. Accent Colour.

ROOM COLOUR

What is an Accent Colour?

Put simply it's an optional splash of colour that is added to a scheme to draw the eye and make that particular item stand out. It should be a complementary colour. It's usually the fourth or fifth colour to be added to a scheme and will be used in a couple of areas around a room. It's noticeably used most in neutral colour schemes, where short sharp burst of colours improve the overall design.

Accent Colour is usually, but not always, a bright colour. Hot Orange, Scarlet, Royal Blue, Violet, Lime Green, Golden Yellow, Cerise Pink... all those colours that people find a bit too much to use in great quantities or on large surfaces. Accent colours will be used in cushions, mirrors, rugs, throws, lighting, table lamps. Accent colour is also used to bring rooms together. So, using the same 'burnt orange' in curtains in one room, a rug in another room and cushions in a further room is an example of using accent colour to progress a scheme around a property.

Let's look at some room colour schemes to see where and how a palette of colours fit together..

In the 4 colour scheme seen here, **on the right**:

Colour 1 – this is the deep Fire Pink of the curtain print and the armchair.

Colour 2 – this is the coffee coloured Broncho; shown in rug and the flooring as well as the table lamps at the far end of the room.

Colour 3 – this is the lighter Silverflake of the wooden doors and the sofa.

Neutral Base – this base is a rich Cream as shown on the walls and the base of the curtains.

In this scenario, is Colour 3 an Accent Colour? Not really as it doesn't have the 'bright' unexpected aspect and a sofa is a large item. The white/cream sofa has been chosen because it's blends, not to add an 'accent'.

ROOM COLOUR

In the 4 colour scheme seen here **below**, we see more neutrals than colour, but the scheme is warm and inviting:

Colour 1 – this is the Grey of the sofa and armchairs; also echoed in the seating in the room beyond.

Colour 2 – this is the warm wood of the unit and the frame of the mirror. The pairing of grey and orange tones is very popular.

Colour 3 – this is the deep sand colour of the wooden flooring.

Neutral Base – this base is Off White as shown on the walls and curtains.

Below:

Colour 1 – this is the Burnt Orange of the sofa, the cushions on the opposite seating area and the woven rug (despite the rug being textured, it still brings colour in).

Colour 2 – this is the Chartreuse shown in the seat pads on the opposite seating area and picked up with the brass in the chandelier

Colour 3 – this is the muted Blue that you see in the side table, plain cushion and cushion print. This scheme was chosen to not overdo it with one or more colours but to use warm muted shades altogether against a cool background.

Neutral Base – this base is Pale Cirrus as shown on the walls and in the two armchairs.

Colours and Palettes

PINK

Because of its connotations, the fact that pink is the most widely used colour for clothes, toys and any other product for girls, Pink has been avoided for many years. Adding a warmth of colour to a cool neutral should be seen as gold dust but instead it is feared and overlooked. Italianate pink or a soft terracotta are beautiful to work with.

Depending on what type of colours you mix together, you get a different pink for your interior. The sugary pinks are the reds and whites mixed together. Those dusky pinks with warmer tones have yellow added to them so you achieve an almost 'sandstone pink'. However, if you add Brown, the pink becomes deeper and moodier. It just depends on what mood you want to go for.

'PINK MAKES THE BOYS WINK', AS THE OLD SAYING GOES…

What should I avoid putting with Pink?

Orange – rarely do bright orange and pink shades look good together – they tend to compete. At least the hot shades do. You will find that terracotta and dusky pink will blend into one another quite well.

Purple – Pink and Purple are too samey. As pink comes from red and purple comes from blue, these two sit side by side comfortably in clothing, but in interior design, they can be overwhelming. Often seen as the masculine and feminine competing, it's better to keep them apart and let other more subtle shades work with pink.

Where to try it:

Living Room - a subtle warm glow will work well in both winter and summer. All those sofas in beige, cream, grey and chocolate won't jar and you'll introduce an elegant air when entertaining.

Top Tip:

Try putting a subtle, pale tint of pink on the ceiling to warm the room up and to counteract harsh overhead lighting.

ROOM COLOUR

PALE PINK

Pale pink (sometimes called Architectural Pink) and grey, seen here, are easy bedfellows. Welcoming visitors with a rosy atmosphere is something that is rarely thought about these days, but I always try to add subtle welcoming colours to my interiors. This pink is Hansel and Gretel from Fired Earth and would work well in a hallway, living room, bathroom or bedroom.

It's worth noting that pale pink works well with stronger colours as well as with the normal range of pastels. Below we see Woad Blue grounding the pale pink. And with it, White Mulberry, a soft cream, is much kinder to the eye than brilliant white for the neutral woodwork. Secondly, Pale Coumarin is a soft yellow that complements the pink whilst Weald Green gives some depth to the scheme. Platinum Pale is there to freshen the palette as the other colours are all very warm.

Clever combinations with Hansel and Gretel:

www.homeconscious.com   25

ROOM COLOUR

CERISE PINK

Cerise pink, seen here as Little Greene's Leather, gives this bedroom bold brightness. With natural light from the double doors, this room looks spectacular in the sunshine. Print curtains in Sunny Yellow add to the uniqueness. Notice how the bed, mirror and skirting are kept sharp in white. Choosing cream for these items would overload the room with warmth but a bright white freshens the scheme. For mature depth, dark wood furniture would also work with these colours. Other tones for this shade include Magenta and Fuchsia.

Don't be afraid to try these shades out; in small passageways, in cloakrooms and on feature walls, if you are bit apprehensive about painting all four walls in this boldest of pinks.

Clever combinations with Leather:

ROOM COLOUR

DUSKY PINK

Perfect for bedrooms, this is a superb colour that is often overlooked for other areas of the home. It works equally well in living rooms and I've used this myself in TV rooms, hallways and passageways.

Seen here is Albany's Coral Rose. Unusually, this has been used on the ceiling, as well as the upper part of the wall above the wood panelling in Nougat. Teamed with vivid lime green soft furnishings, this is a strong combination and not to everyone's taste. Notice how the wood panelling blends seamlessly in with the white units on the left and the neutral carpet has coral undertones to retain a cosy air.

Other shades for this palette of pink include Salmon Pink, Sugar Pink and Soft Terracotta.

Clever Combinations with Coral Rose:

www.homeconscious.com 27

BLUE

Possibly the most widely used colour of all. While the inevitable Blue-Grey is still with us and will continue to be for a while to come, other blues have been coming forward to claim their space. Generally thought of as a cold colour for interiors, Blue can work incredibly well in bedrooms and hallways.

It's still a masculine colour, but that is gradually changing as more women use blue for their businesses and refuse to be bound by society's use of pink for girls. Perhaps Blue's reputation for coolness, serenity and calmness also stirs those emotions from within us. We would all like to be calmer, cooler and more serene in our daily lives!

USE 'ONCE IN A BLUE MOON' - SOMETHING NO INTERIOR DESIGNER SHOULD SAY ABOUT BLUE.

What should I avoid putting with Blue?

Red – unless you're creating a national flag or a fast food brand, I'd steer clear of these two together!

Purple – Mid Blue and Mid Purple are, again, too 'samey'. Put together they can darken a room quite considerably. Strangely this does not apply if you are using a darker blue and a pale lilac – or a deep purple and a pale blue. It seems the contrast of depth makes the shades work well together. See below for details.

Where to try it:

Study - a business like blue conveys the right amount of formality for a study. Whether it is Navy, Airforce or Ice Blue, the base shade of blue will fit well within most businesses. Think Facebook and LinkedIn!

Top Tip:

A trend to watch out for is the shade of Smalt. This is a strong and deep Royal Blue that was often used on metal railings surrounding houses. It's a mix of crushed blue glass and lapis lazuli with other natural minerals. One to watch out for!

ROOM COLOUR

ICE BLUE

Also related to Pale Blue and Powder Blue, Ice Blue is in constant use in interiors. Seen here in this drawing room is Airlane Blue from Sanderson.

Don't be afraid to use Ice Blue both in bedrooms and particularly in girls bedrooms. It can be incredibly feminine so don't dismiss it.

But it's mainly seen as a cool and refined colour; here it is used to convey calmness and elegance. Print curtains in creams, blues and gold shades lend themselves well to this room with its double aspect windows and warm wooden flooring. The main sofa is also in ice blue to reinforce the cool palette.

Clever combinations with Airlane Blue:

ROOM COLOUR

TURQUOISE

Bright, uncompromising and bold, Turquoise is a shade that is being used more and more in our homes. With such a shade, you can afford to accentuate the blue with a bright white. Pictured here is Little Greene's Gentle Sky with Farrow & Ball's All White. Because you are not in a hallway long enough, (it's essentially a place to walk through, not spend any time), it's a great idea to use a bold colour such as turquoise all over. This hallway could have been dark and flat with a neutral but the blue keeps it fresh and current. Maintaining the varnished banister and the carpet neutral keeps this hallway warm and comfortable.

Don't be afraid to go for a deeper hue either. Many stately homes embrace Turquoise as it is a perfect foil for antique wood and golden gilt frames.

Clever combinations with Gentle Sky:

ROOM COLOUR

AIRFORCE BLUE

Essentially a Blue-Grey, this is one of the most popular shades used today. Because of it subtlety, Blue-Grey, or Grey-Blue is often used in areas of high traffic; notably hallways and kitchens. Airforce Blue and its lighter brother seen here, James, both by Little Greene is used here with Shirting, with the banister retained in natural wood. The painted console, just seen in the left foreground, is in Chocolate. The effect is smart and does not overpower the eye - you barely notice the purple undertones.

Cobalt Blue: Colbalt Blue sits between Airforce Blue and Royal Blue. But it has that richness and depth that Royal Blue doesn't have. It's a smarter hue and tends to be used in masculine interiors above all else. It's an unusual colour to see because of this - remember most interiors are decided by women who tend to steer away from overtly masculine shades.

Clever combinations with James:

ROOM COLOUR

NAVY

Yacht Blue Lt and its darker brother, Indigo Blue, are universally smart. Sophisticated and grown up, Navy is mostly seen as a masculine shade, though it should not be discounted when choosing a shade for busy family rooms. Here it is in a bedroom teamed with gunmetal grey and Chartreuse Yellow.

Notice how the decorative art prints really 'pop' from the dark wall, despite their dark frames. It's worth noting that Navy can be used most anywhere, in any part of the house; it's almost a neutral in itself. Use on feature walls – particularly where you won't be walking next to it or touching it with fingers. Like most dark shades, Navy shows fingerprints, grease, smudges and scuffs easily.

Clever combinations with Yacht Blue Lt:

ROOM COLOUR

AQUA

Aqua – that strange shade that is technically half-way between Blue and Green is a very easy and comfortable shade to work with. It never offends, and looks equally good with both stronger colours and flat neutrals. Here, Little Greene's Pale Berlin back wall is teamed with Regency Blue to really add some modernity and youth to this kitchen.

Use this shade to convey calmness and serenity. Don't be fooled into thinking this is too strong a colour for a room. Remember, carpets, window dressings and furniture will break up the freshness.

Specialist wipe-clean paint should be used if you're decorating a kitchen as here, and have little or no tiles as a splashback or upstand. Water gets everywhere!

Clever combinations with Pale Berlin:

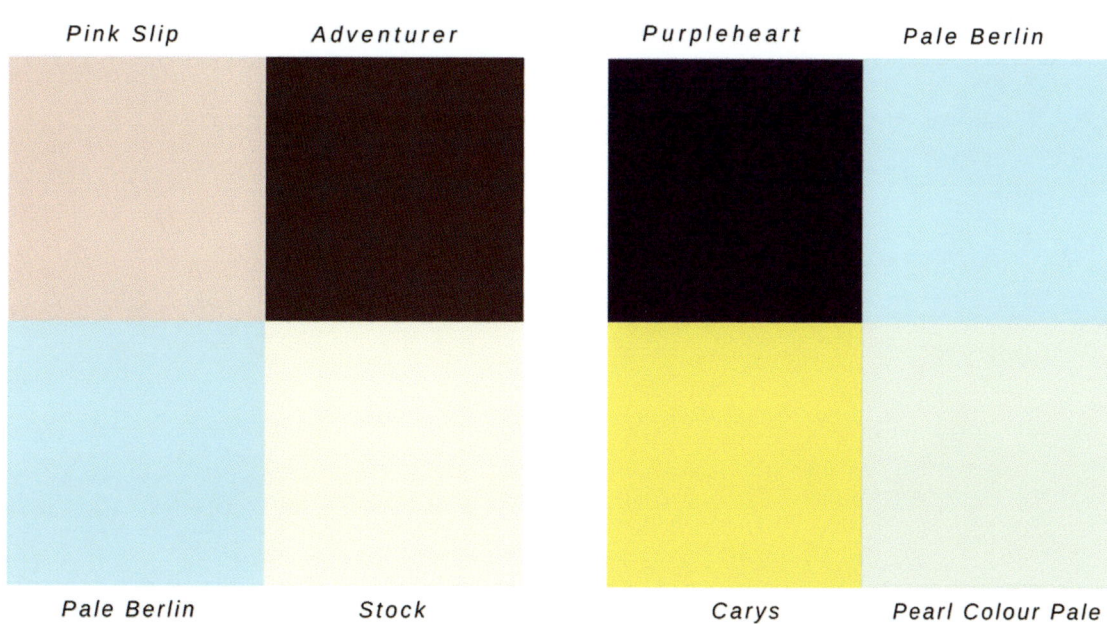

ROOM COLOUR

PEACOCK BLUE

Peacock Blue has tones of green that make it ideal for many properties. Used by the individual who is confident yet measured, it's a shade that adds gravitas to colour schemes that otherwise would remain neutral. One of the jewel colours, Little Greene's Canton, seen here, is a fabulous colour for an otherwise white room that kitchens often are. Because high traffic areas are often repainted more often, darker colours are often the best option when looking to inject colour. The woodwork, painted in Shirting, has been left pure white to maintain sharpness. A single stool in Baked Cherry is echoed in the bowls and linen towel. With a colour like Canton, don't be afraid to warm the shade up. Or go darker still with other shades. Sometimes deeper shades like this need to bounce off other deeper shades to really show their potential.

Clever combinations with Canton:

ROOM COLOUR

DUSTY BLUE

Dusty Blue (or even Dusky Blue) is right next to Airforce Blue on the colour charts. The difference is the amount of grey perceived in the shade by the eye.

This very elegant living room is in Little Greene's Celestial Blue. Once a Regency colour, it can look green in some lights. It lends itself well to any room in the house, working well with warmer, richer shades (seen here with a Bronze Red picture frame) as well as with deeper shades such as Marine Blue, shown beneath the dado rail.

Both Oranges and Greys are good partner for Dusty Blue. Use them in both lighter and darker shades to treat the eye!

Clever combinations with Celestial Blue:

ROOM COLOUR

POWDER BLUE

Farrow & Ball's Lulworth Blue is used to great effect in this bedroom. Bright and crisp with All White, this owner has decided to showcase the colour by not distracting the eye with curtains or blinds. Instead, a mushroom coloured carpet and bedspread are used with rustic wooden furniture to ground the scheme. Spot colour, in the way of a Clementine table lamp jolts the eye.

I've used Lulworth Blue before for nurseries and also for period properties as it's a good true blue and very much like the Mediterranean sky. Because this blue is very cool, it's a good idea to team it with some warmer tones such as yellows, pinks and oranges. This pairing will benefit both colours in your scheme.

Clever combinations with Lulworth Blue:

RED

A very underused colour, Red, used wisely can really make your scheme stand out. From bright Scarlet to plush Crimson, Red is a colour not for the faint hearted. Used extensively in large country houses for its warmth and it boldness, Red is a colour steeped in history.

Today, Red is used in Dining Rooms to give character and warmth, in Studies to show seriousness and in Bars to increase relaxation. It also acts as a great backdrop for art - think of all the museums that use it - as it is the perfect foil for monochrome artwork. Historically reds were made up of yellows and pinks so it is perhaps not surprising that these two colours are often teamed with Red in an interior. Red-Pink naturally stems from Red anyway but don't be put off from using Red in its purest form when you look at choosing your scheme.

'PAINT THE TOWN RED!'

What should I avoid putting with Red?

Royal Blue – unless you're creating a national flag or a fast food brand, I'd steer clear of these two!

Purple – Blue and Purple are, again, too alike. Put together they can darken a room quite considerably. You need more of a contrast. Preferably a cooler contrast. Try Green.

Where to try it:

Cloakroom - a small room can make just an impact as a large room. Warm and welcoming, but practical and comfortable; red is an ideal colour to use in a guest cloakroom.

Top Tip:

Add in gold tones into your red room for a grand and rich scheme. Don't be afraid to add antiques and gilt to the accessories. Red can handle all manner of traditionality.

ROOM COLOUR

RED

Farrow & Ball's Charlotte's Locks, seen here, is used to give this living room an audacious air.

Whilst the furniture is modern and monochrome, the ceiling in All White and the white tiled floor doesn't allow this room to get dark.

Scarlet and its sisters, Vermillion and Tomato Red are the brightest but warmest colours you can use.

It's a very young look, much used in children's rooms and cloakrooms. Indeed, Scarlett as a colour is so bold it is best to team it with neutrals in order not to feel overwhelmed.

Clever combinations with Charlotte's Locks:

Charlotte's Locks   *Pelt*

Farrow's Cream   *White Tie*

Charlotte's Locks   *Elephant's Breath*

London Clay   *Slipper Satin*

ROOM COLOUR

CRIMSON

Crimson is a deep red that was traditionally used in gentleman's libraries. Here, it has been used to its full effect. By placing Little Greene's Deep Space Blue, effectively as a cornice, the Bronze Red is not as overwhelming as it could be. Notice how the warm effect is heightened by adding in a russet brown leather armchair and 50's wooden table. With a white panel door and skirting in Yellow Pink this interior says unique and creative.

Use this colour sparingly if you are unsure. I've used it in bathrooms and passageways to great effect when the colour is right but the client is hesitating!

Clever combinations with Bronze Red:

| Bronze red | Salix | | Bronze Red | Linnet |
| Hollyhock | Julie's Dream | | French Grey | Stock |

www.homeconscious.com

39

ROOM COLOUR

BURGUNDY

Burgundy has a lot more brown within it than Crimson and for this reason it gives a muddy and subversive tone to a room.

Here, Little Greene's Ashes Of Roses has been used both on the wall and the woodwork – an effect that is not often seen in houses – though commercial premises seem to like this technique. Because of its depth and warmth, you can afford to be a little zingy when pairing it up. A pale lime sofa accentuates both shades whist the table, in Light Peachblossom joins the two colours together.

Burgundy is a good choice for homes that see a lot of cloudy and wet weather. The deep tones seem to be made for this type of natural light. Use with lots of gold and copper accessories!

Clever combinations with Ashes of Roses:

Ashes of Roses	Pitcairn	Ashes of Roses	Trumpet
Thai Sapphire	White Lead	Regency Fawn	Slaked Lime

ROOM COLOUR

MAROON

Maroon has many purple undertones and is used in many regal interiors – especially in high traffic areas. Here, Adventurer by Little Greene is used on wood panelling behind a bed. The two neutrals of this scheme are kept light and fresh in order to accentuate the warmth of the maroon. Whilst the floor is kept bare and understated in Linen Wash, the side table, in China Clay really stands out. This could be very stark, but for the tactile, printed silk of the headboard and crisp cotton bed linen.

Again, notice how the window frame and sill have also been painted in Adventurer. This is commonly done in hotels and other commercial properties. Use Maroon in studies, hallways, passageways and cloakrooms for an intellectual mood.

Clever combinations with Adventurer:

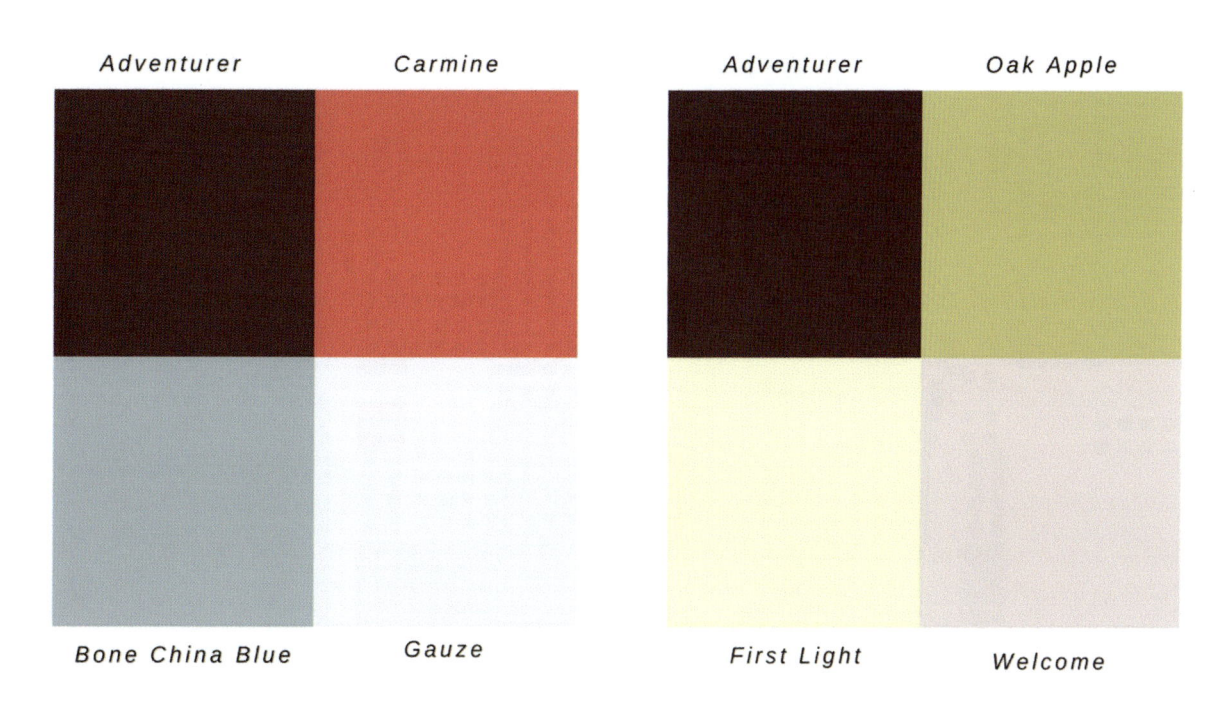

| Adventurer | Carmine | | Adventurer | Oak Apple |
| Bone China Blue | Gauze | | First Light | Welcome |

YELLOW

Yellow is the brightest colour, bar white, that you can use in your interior. Universally seen as a happy, sunny colour, it's used to brighten up dark spaces, to bring fun into children's rooms and to give depth and richness to formal rooms.

It's always been a favourite colour of mine and if used correctly, it can really make your scheme unique, something most designers can only dream of. Whilst it's not a popular colour these days, it will show your intellectual side if you're brave enough to use it. Feature walls are somewhere to start but don't discount painting an entire room with lemon, acacia, buttermilk, golden yellow or daffodil. Be brave!

> **'SOME PAINTERS TRANSFORM THE SUN INTO A YELLOW SPOT; OTHERS TRANSFORM A YELLOW SPOT INTO THE SUN' – PABLO PICASSO**

What should I avoid putting with Yellow?

Pale Pink – unless you're creating a nursery and it has good natural light. Pink and yellow can appear very sugary if the paler shades are used.

Red – be careful that red and yellow don't compete for attention in your scheme. Using these colours in furniture can be lovely, but paint colours can overdo the warmth of a room.

Where to try it:

Kitchen - whether bold and searing or delicate and subtle, a yellow kitchen says family, happiness and busyness. It will go well with most units and can be made to look traditional or modern - depending on the shade or tint.

Top Tip:

If painting a pale yellow onto walls - go for a dark creamy colour for the woodwork to bathe the room in warmth.

ROOM COLOUR

GOLDEN YELLOW

Yellow Pink by Little Greene has a name that contradicts. However, it is one of the most effective warmer yellows that you can use. Because of its warmth, a cooler and darker contrast is used to anchor the eye. It's a great choice for walls.

To great effect, this door frame and skirting has been painted Lamp Black to stand out against the yellow. Notice how the door itself is kept light so that your eye is not overwhelmed with rich colours.

Golden Yellow is a somewhat underused colour in metropolitan homes but is found extensively in period homes around the United Kingdom. It works equally well with both modern and antique furniture and for a really elegant finish, look to a patterned/printed rug that picks up golden tones.

Clever combinations with Golden Yellow:

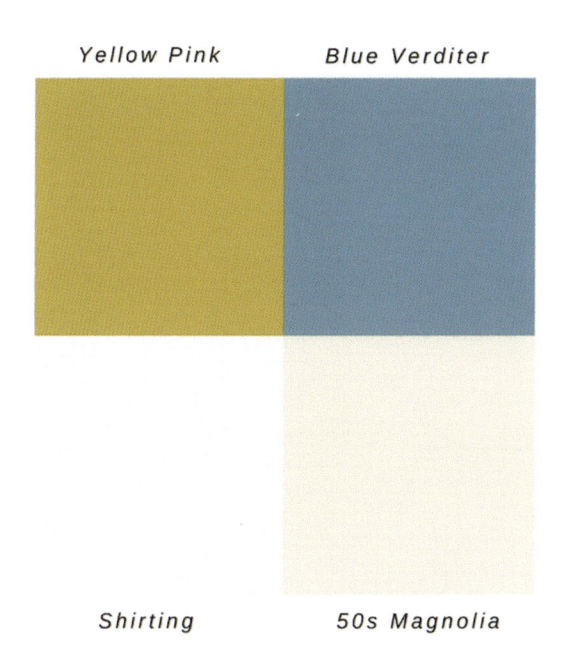

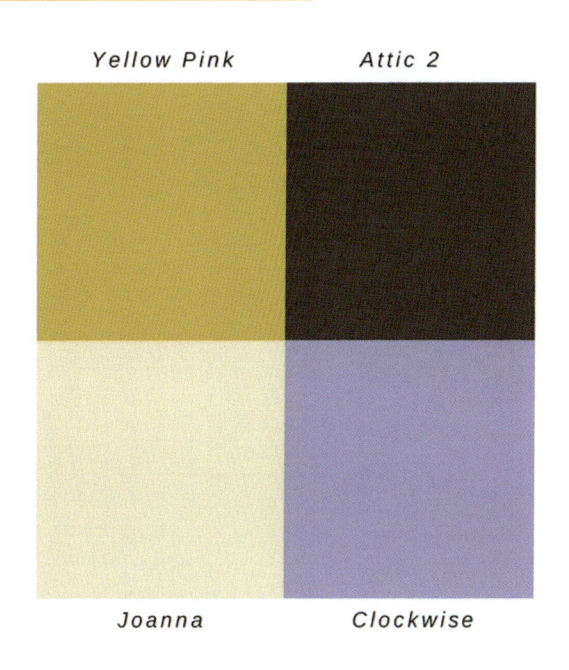

Yellow Pink	Blue Verditer		Yellow Pink	Attic 2
Shirting	50s Magnolia		Joanna	Clockwise

ROOM COLOUR

LEMON

Bright, searing lemon yellow, sometimes called Acacia Yellow is a joy to behold in properties. Done right, it can transform a property from safe and boring to bold and impressive.

Here the acidic tones of Trumpet from Little Greene are heightened by the ceiling, dado and woodwork in Shirting.

Despite the natural wood of the table and flooring, this is a room that you can't ignore. The scheme is carried through to the sitting room beyond. This scheme is very classical – demonstrated by the style of the table and chairs and light fitting. But Trumpet would work equally well in more modern interiors. Try it with orange, grey and purple for maximum impact.

Clever combinations with Trumpet:

Trumpet   *Pale Cirrus*   *Trumpet*   *New Mauve*

Silica White   *Olive Colour*   *Linen Wash*   *Starling*

ROOM COLOUR

PRIMROSE

Primrose, that very prettiest shade of yellow is currently making a comeback in interiors.

Still giving a nod to neutrals but very clearly from the yellow palette, Primrose, is a wise choice for any room in the house having cool as well as warm tones. It's a great choice for girls rooms for those that don't want to adhere to the stereotypical pink that girls are subjected to.

A very good mood lifter, it works very well with bolder shades as well as pastels. Here, Custard has been used very effectively in a small stairway.

Clever combinations with Custard:

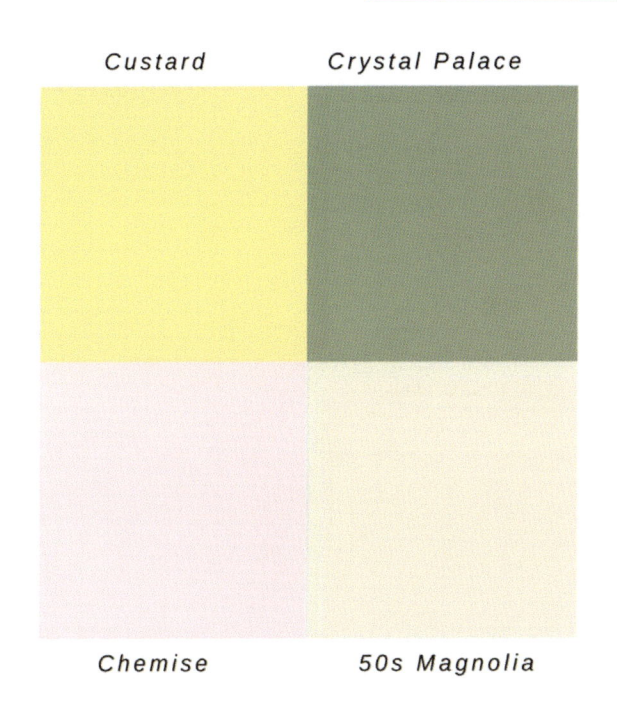

Custard	Crystal Palace		Custard	Meadow Violet
Chemise	50s Magnolia		Hammock	Stock

BROWN

Brown – the colour of chocolate, coffee and the earth. For some people this is all they need! Brown is a colour that we cannot ignore as so much of it surrounds us whether it's the trees that line our streets or the earth that our food grows in. It's also the frames that our furniture is made from and the colour of our hair, eyes and skin.

But in interior terms – it's had a bad deal over the last few years. It had a resurgence in the 1970's when it was teamed with oranges and yellows, with bold prints and coloured glass adding to the darker hues of the decade. Perhaps this is the reason that it has been largely ignored for Grey over the past 30 years or so. This is not to say that its lighter cousins such as taupe and mushroom haven't been popular – they have. But they are not true Brown. There is a richness to Brown. Its depth and naturalness make it a compelling argument for interiors today – although progress is slow.

But I wouldn't discount it too soon – variants of Brown are popping up such as leather and copper and a return to the deeper tones of peat and hazelnut are on the cards.

'CHOCOLATE IS ALWAYS THE ANSWER..'

What should I avoid putting with Brown?

Orange – unless you're creating a 70's vibe in your home! Although these two colours work well – the 70's connotations will still be uppermost in most people's minds.

Grey – one dark neutral is more than enough, especially if you intend to have wooden flooring or wooden furniture.

Where to try it:

Landing - practical yet stoic, Brown is a great colour to add to those passages that see wear and tear every day. Add Brown to feature walls as a backdrop to family photos and momentos.

Top Tip:

If you're really brave, a warm blue or red on the the woodwork can accentuate and lift the brown from the walls.

ROOM COLOUR

BROWN

A rich deep brown sits comfortably in this living room with a large picture window. By using Den Lt by Sanderson the walls, this room becomes cosy, practical and warm. The Venetian blinds give a pared down and modern air. Whether during strong sunlight or a blizzard outside, this room will continue to feel cosy and comfortable.

Yellow is a good shade for brown along with warm neutrals as seen here – think of all those yellow blossom trees that work so well in nature for inspiration. Alternatively, look to those pastels that you would never think of – lilac, peach, mint green…they all become mature with a deep brown to anchor them.

Clever combinations to use with Den Lt:

| Den Lt | Window Blue | Den Lt | Mad King George |
| Queen Anne Green Lt | Winter White | Silver Dust | Matterhorn |

ROOM COLOUR

TAN

Seen mostly in commercial properties, Tan, or as shown here, Bath Stone by Little Greene, is also underused in the modern home. Thought of as too dark for some rooms, it nonetheless gives an air of sophistication and intelligence when used in the home. Here it is seen in a bedroom. No concession to a light airy feel has been given.

Indeed the dark wooden furniture and feminine bed linen increase the mature feel. Often, using darker accessories can often make the walls appear much lighter – even when the wall colour is not a lighter shade to begin with. Bear in mind how much light you get into rooms that are painted in this shade. Light bulbs will also make a difference so test carefully in daylight and during the evening.

Clever combinations with Bath Stone:

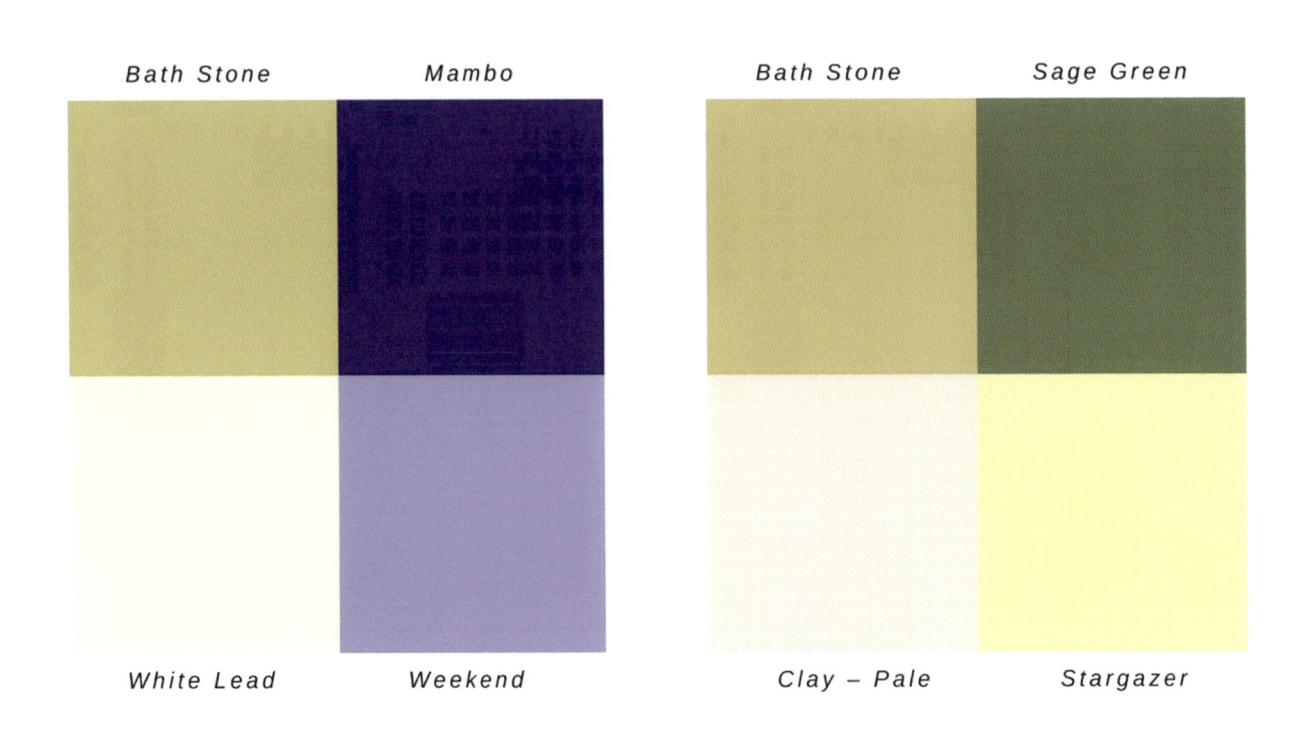

| Bath Stone | Mambo | | Bath Stone | Sage Green |
| White Lead | Weekend | | Clay – Pale | Stargazer |

48 www.homeconscious.com

ROOM COLOUR

BEIGE, TAUPE, FAWN...

All of the variants of Brown that make up the neutral shades of Ecru, Beach Beige, Fawn 10, Ivory Sand, etc should be used when needed, but not in every room in the house!

Invariably, warm browns, sands and beiges will be used in furniture and flooring so using a colour on the walls is preferable and will lift your scheme considerably.

However, if an all neutral colour scheme is insisted upon, then you will need to add in lots of texture with the soft furnishings that you choose. Bouclé armchairs, printed curtains or blinds and abstract-geometric headboards (as seen here) will all help to lift the scheme. It is best to create either a lightness and calmness of the neutral shade, seen here in this bedroom, or to evoke a monochrome palette with darker wood that will appear more formal and mature.

...AND CREAM

Cream is a colour that works well in any scheme but has the unfortunate reputation of 'boring'. Because Magnolia was so popular over the last few decades, Cream has a bad reputation and is often overlooked. That said, it has been repackaged over the years into a multitude of names such as White Lead, Clunch, Oyster and Imperial Ivory.

It's warm, practical, unthreatening and safe. Try using some of its richer tones; Dorset Cream, Creamerie, Aged Ivory, Farrow's Cream if you want more warmth in your scheme. All these will be less insipid than the lighter 'off white' that you see everywhere today and will give a depth to any artwork hung on it. Consider using a colour for your woodwork if you go for Cream on the walls. Be contrary and don't follow the crowd!

ORANGE

Orange being one of the boldest colours you can choose for a home seems to polarise people. Until you speak to them about the various shades that there are to choose from that is.

Burnt Orange is liked, Peach less so. Tangerine is to fear whilst Apricot is to welcome. Until you see and try orange in action, it is hard to envisage this shade in your home. But the gentle shade of Terracotta lends itself well to a variety of styles and it's perhaps here that you should start when considering choosing orange for your scheme.

Take your time and try on woodwork, feature walls and accessories if you really want to add orange, but worry that a whole room will overpower you. Layering with furniture is a good idea in front of orange walls. It will help break up the bold wall behind it.

'DOES ANYTHING RHYME WITH ORANGE?'

What should I avoid putting with Orange?

Red – it might work for fresh peppers, but these two are just too powerful together.

Brown – unless you're going for a 70s vibe – steer clear of these two together.

Where to try it:

Conservatories or Sun Rooms - a great excuse for bright orange florals and hot house botanicals. Use sparingly around a room to add colour to walls and to highlight windows and doors.

Top Tip:

Be careful not to add too much of a Mexican influence when using orange. You don't want to look like a holiday villa! Anchor your Orange with cool greys, crisp whites and deep crimsons.

TERRACOTTA

Terracotta is such a rich and beautiful colour, it's surprising it's not used more.

Terra di Sienna by Little Greene, is seen here paired with cream, white and the natural elements of wood and exposed brick. It's a colour that is by no means untraditional but it's seen as very much a modern shade – especially with the recent resurgence of Copper.

Some shades can appear pink and are utterly charming to use. Other tones are sunnier with yellow strains. Look carefully at your furniture, particularly wooden items – you don't want everything to disappear into the wall. One of the most popular pairings puts orange with grey - a very modern look and a good choice for terracotta.

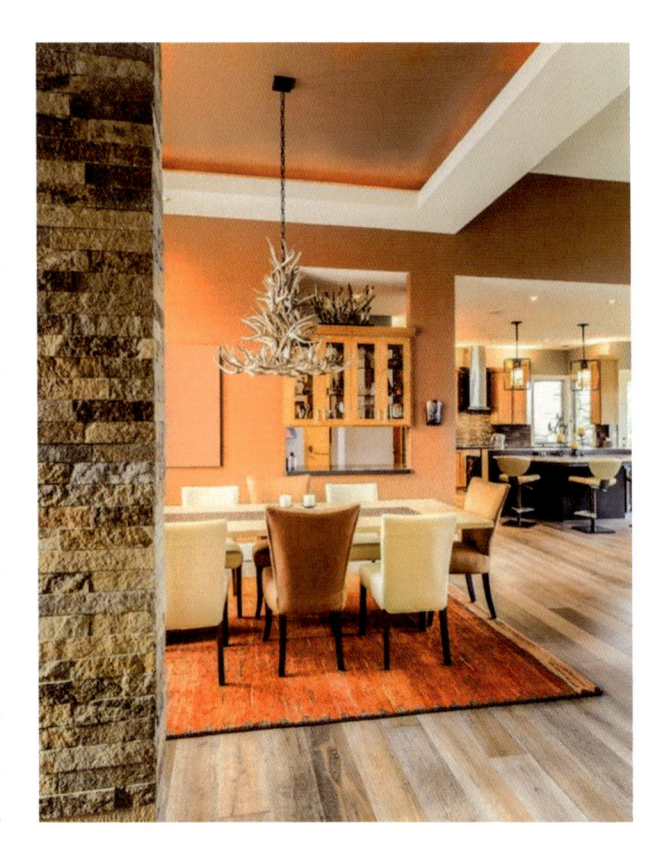

Clever combinations with Terra di Sienna:

Terra di Sienna	Rusling		Terra di Sienna	Blue Verditer
Ivory	Beauvais Lilac		Bone China Blue Mid	Old Paper II

ROOM COLOUR

BURNT ORANGE

Burnt Orange or Heat, as seen here, is the strongest, deepest Orange you can get. Very Mediterranean, it will need 3, possibly 4 coats on the walls to really do it justice. Once applied, it will immediately make a statement and will continue to do so for months if not years.

It's not as violent as red and for that reason it is used more in homes.

Pair it with white, gold and mahogany as seen here. When choosing other colours to put with Burnt Orange, you should look at both the warmer shades and the cooler shades as seen below. Because it's such a mighty colour, keep deep reds, purples and blues away to ensure that the orange takes centre stage and isn't competing with other strong shades.

Clever combinations with Heat:

| *Heat* | *Julie's Dream* | | *Heat* | *Eau de Nil* |
| *Mushroom* | *Stock* | | *Whitening* | *Acorn* |

www.homeconscious.com

GREEN

After Blue, Green is the most widely used of the all the colours. Restful and yet fresh, it lends itself to every kind of interior. Its shades are so varied that it's possible to team it with every other colour there is. It is perhaps because of nature that we are so drawn to green. Like Blue, it is 'life giving' and is seen in every country on earth to be representative of newness and the birth of Spring.

Nevertheless, it is hard to get the right colour as the choice is so huge. Too cold a green and suddenly you need to inject a variety of warmer shades, too sludgy and your room will appear dusty. Take care to sharpen duller colours with bold accents or brights.

If in doubt, pick a particular tone and layer lighter or darker shades and tints around it so that there are no punctuation points, just a wave of undulating colour.

'THE GREEN GREEN GRASS OF HOME..'

What should I avoid putting with Green?

Red and white – if you have chosen a spring or grass green, adding red and white will be too much like a national flag!

Brown – at least on its own. The two colours together can be a little too reminiscent of nature.

Where to try it:

Hallways - adding a dado rail and perhaps panelling below in a subtle green can enable you to use some striking wallpaper above. This would really make a statement!

Top Tip:

Work through blues and greens to get a good flow throughout your home. Concentrating on three or four shades in your home can be the easiest place to start. You can then add upholstery and curtains to brighten the palette up.

ROOM COLOUR

PEA GREEN

Little Greene's Citrine, seen here, is a fabulous colour for walls. Paired with Slaked Lime, it's a colour that demands simplicity and a lighter shade to play off. The dining table accessories in Atomic Red keep this scheme current – and as we all know, red is the opposite of green so the two together are a winning combination.

Because Citrine is such a bold colour and is essentially a 1950's shade, you can mix it up a little when creating your palette. Either go with the warmer pink tones of the first example below; or go with the sharper tones of the second palette.

It's good to look at some of these bolder and more unusual greens about. Try and think of the mood you are trying to create when picking out a shade. Let that be your guide.

Clever combinations with Citrine:

Citrine	Shrimp Pink		Citrine	Mister David
China Clay	Clay		Rolling Fog Pale	Linnet

ROOM COLOUR

GARDEN GREEN

Garden Green by Little Greene is a splendidly practical green that works well in large houses with high ceilings. Seen here in a typical hallway, the shade immediately conveys distance and space as your eye is taken down the passage to the back of the property. It is teamed here with Whitening – one of my favourite colours to use on woodwork. A Georgian colour, Whitening is a rich white/cream that looks fantastic with white, cream or colour walls equally. Not harsh like brilliant white, it is my go-to colour for woodwork in period properties.

Hallways are one of the most important areas in a property. They are the first thing that you walk into and the first (and sometimes the only) part that visitors see. Using colour (or wallpaper for that matter) in a hallway is very sophisticated and if you are going to set the standard for colour in your home – this is where to start.

Clever combinations with Garden Green:

Garden Green	Beauvais Lilac		Garden Green	Batsman
Rustling	Invisible Green		Indian Sand	Mirror

ROOM COLOUR

GRASS GREEN

Fired Earth's Mad King George is a bright green that is not for the faint hearted. Paired here with chairs in Cochineal red, the green really does this room justice. Notice how the artwork works well with the bolder colour on the walls. Again, this is why art galleries and museums use this green to great effect.

Country houses also use this shade to show off antiques and artwork in gilt frames. Grass Green and gold is a winning combination for the eye. I've often used it when renovating large houses that need to convey heritage and history. Red and Green are opposite colours, so they complement each other well - but take care that a small room doesn't get overwhelmed by all the 'primary' colours you choose.

Clever combinations with Mad King George:

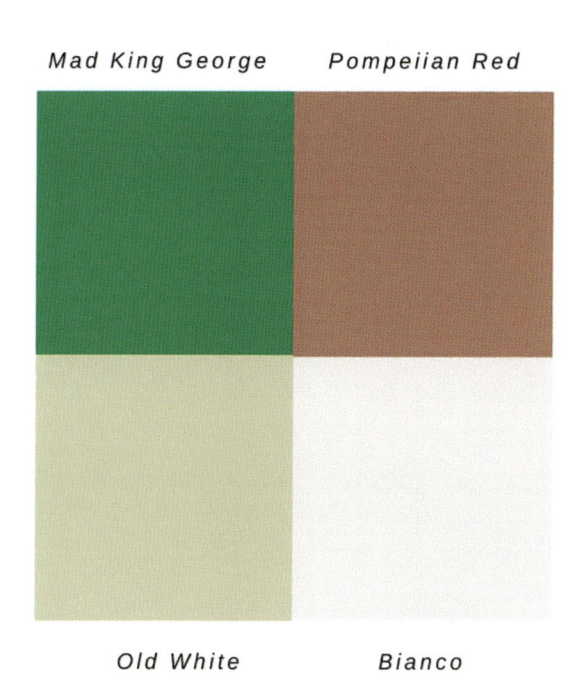

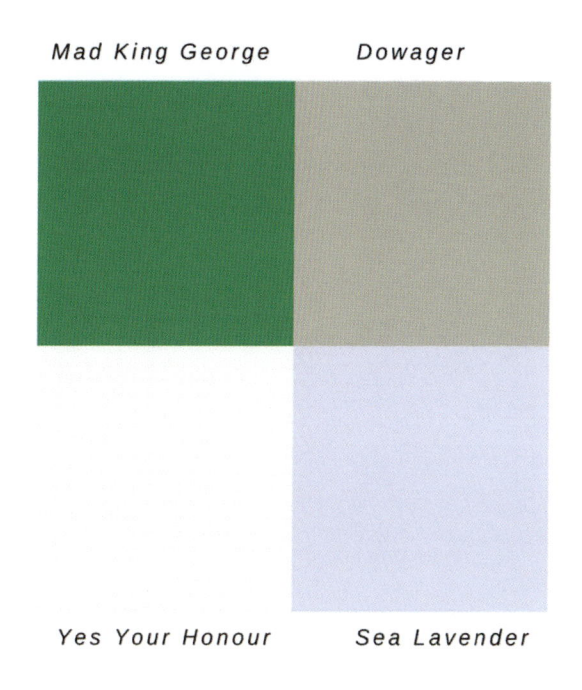

Mad King George	Pompeiian Red
Old White	Bianco

Mad King George	Dowager
Yes Your Honour	Sea Lavender

www.homeconscious.com

ROOM COLOUR

DUSKY GREEN

Dusky Green, like Dusky Blue, is a popular colour all over the world. Seen here is Little Greene's Pea Green. Used on these bookcases, door and frame, this is a lesson on applying colour to woodwork. Too many of us use white or at the very least, a cream on our woodwork. But this goes to show how effective colour can be when transitioning from one room to another.

Through the door we see White Lead Dark on the walls and White Lead Deep on the low wall paneling and window architrave; all the White Lead shades are lovely actually. It's worth building up depth of tones with the same colour in rooms if you don't want to make a statement with your paint.

Clever combinations with Pea Green:

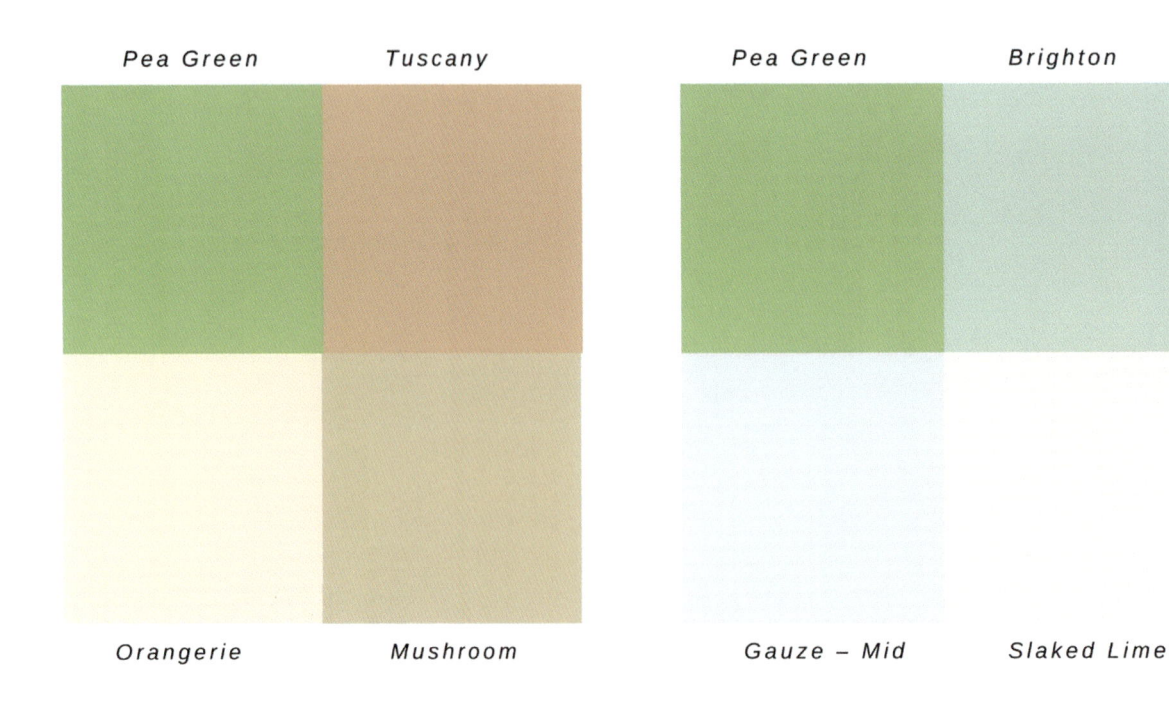

Pea Green	Tuscany		Pea Green	Brighton
Orangerie	*Mushroom*		*Gauze – Mid*	*Slaked Lime*

ROOM COLOUR

TEAL GREEN

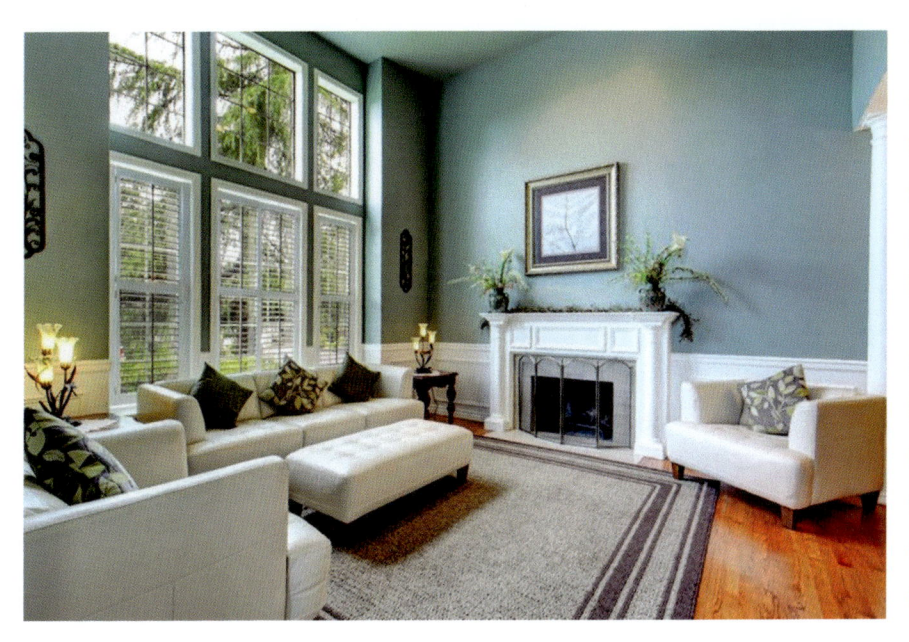

Teal is that in-between colour – is it Blue or is it Green? This depends on the shade but for the sake of argument, I've put it here in the Green section!

Sanderson's Danbury, seen here, is shown to marvellous effect by using simple leather sofas and omitting any fussy window dressing.

Letting the light flood in lightens the paint colour considerably but it still keeps its beautiful sea green depth. This shade of teal can take prettier shades of coral or stronger shades of purple (both seen below) - depending on what mood you want to create.

Clever combinations with Danbury:

Danbury	Coral Shadow		Danbury	Boulder White
Sand Tan	Marshmallow Snow		Turtle Dove	Purpleheart

www.homeconscious.com

ROOM COLOUR

LIME GREEN

Pale Lime from Little Greene is not quite neon. Used almost always in modern interiors rather than period properties, it lends itself to minimal furniture of the retro variety as seen here. If you want to use this shade then I advise using shades to temper it so that it warms rather than shocks.

Keep your furniture simple and again, use other warm shades with this colour so that the walls don't shout at you. Not for the faint hearted!

Clever combinations with Pale Lime:

| Pale Lime | Raspberry Cream | | Pale Lime | Baked Cherry |
| Moonlit Green Lt | Hollyhock | | Slaked Lime | Rolling Fog |

ROOM COLOUR

OLIVE GREEN

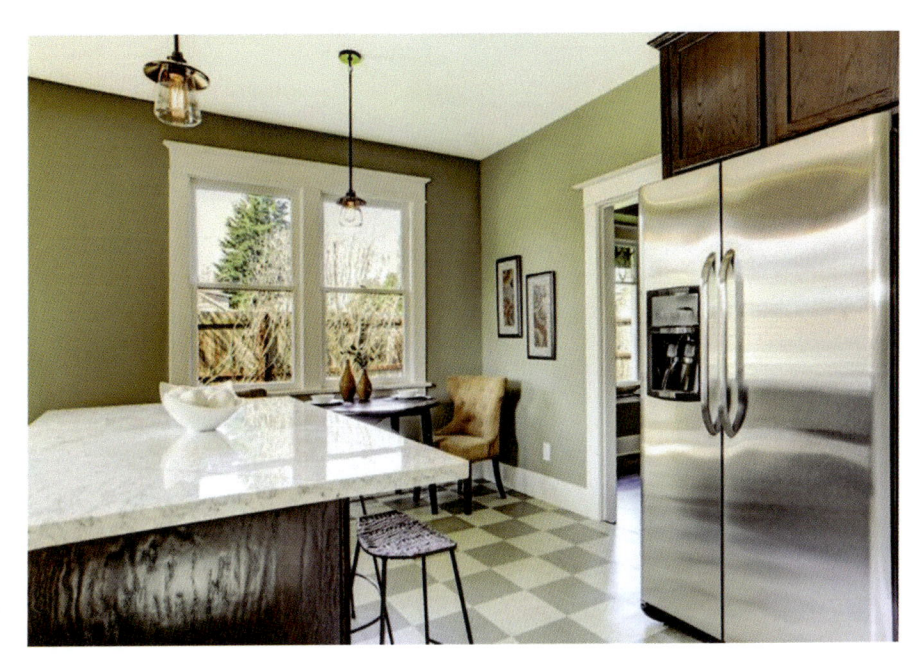

Olive Oil is one of the most popular shades of green today. Seen as sophisticated and smart, yet fresh and classic, olive green exemplifies modern decor today. It's a shade that complements strong contrasting shades like purple but also a plethora of neutrals that it is often teamed with. Here you see it in a smart, modern kitchen.

This is what's great about using colour on your walls – the sharp yet cosy nature of these shades and finishes together make you want to linger in such a room. It's for this reason that you should look beyond the contrasts of both light and dark for paint colours. Adding tonal shades and complementary materials in steel, stone and wood make this scheme look more rounded and relaxed.

Clever combinations with Olive Oil:

| Olive Oil | Milk Thistle | Olive Oil | Linnet |
| China Clay Mid | Silt | Mushroom | First Light |

PURPLE

Purple – the colour of Royalty. Sometimes seen as too strong for most but it is one of the most individual colours you can choose for your interiors. It is true that you have to tread carefully when choosing the right shade of purple. You either go the whole way and make it your base colour with violet, grape or damson; or you include it subtlety with shades of lavender, lilac or mauve. Either way, it's a shade that stands out and surprises.

These days you tend to see purple more as an accent colour. As a wall colour it's been overlooked as it's very specific. If you do want to try it, go for a lighter shade to begin with to test your hunch - you may be persuaded to go brighter next time!

'PLUM CRAZY..'

What should I avoid putting with Purple?

Pink – this will be very sugary if you team pink with purple. It can only work if you make the two colours at opposite ends of the light spectrum; example violet and pale pink. Otherwise, steer clear.

Tan – unless you want to evoke the thought of sludge and mud, choose a different pairing. Tan and purple will blend together a little too well and with any wood in the room, flooring or otherwise, your colours will not stand out.

Where to try it:

Girls Room - a lilac bedroom can be a unique solution to a home if you want something more neutral and unusual. Add in lemon or mint green to bring a touch of zing.

Top Tip:

Be wary of using too many purples in a scheme. Layering with purple can be troublesome; best to team it with other colours for a cleaner effect.

ROOM COLOUR

LILAC

Lilac is a delicate shade that was very popular in the Edwardian era. Seen here is Fired Earth's Chalk Violet. Perfect for a bedroom, I have also successfully added this into a cloakroom, hallway and conservatory.

Lilac is not so well represented in today's interiors. I am hoping this will change as time goes by because it's an effective hue that works both for men and women, and for young and old alike.

When dreaming up a scheme with Lilac, steer clear of sweet pinks and yellows. Think muted yet strong.

Clever combinations with Chalk Violet:

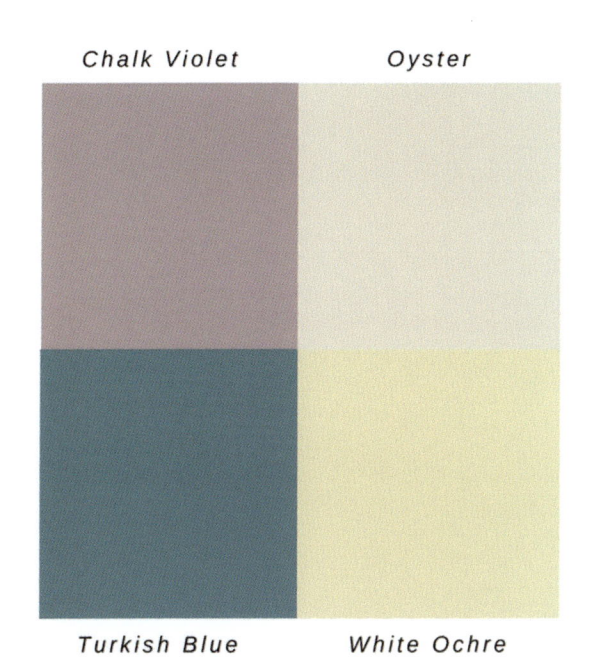

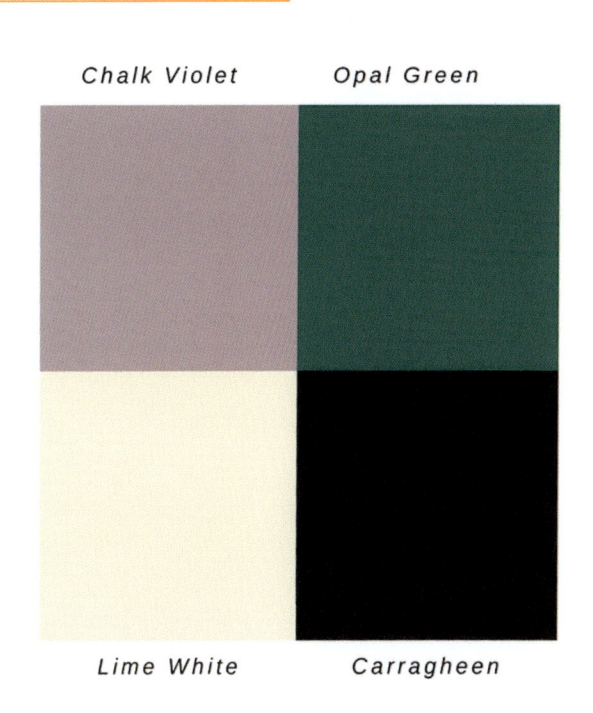

| Chalk Violet | Oyster | | Chalk Violet | Opal Green |
| Turkish Blue | White Ochre | | Lime White | Carragheen |

www.homeconscious.com

ROOM COLOUR

PLUM

Somewhere between Burgundy and Indigo sits Plum. It has a few tones of its own but essentially it's a deep bruised purple that conveys seriousness, formality and wisdom.

Here we see Wild Plum by Sanderson in a sitting room. The stripy sofa doesn't look out of place with its plum and vermillion stripes. Notice how the fireplace, skirting and window frame on the right are picked out in All White by Farrow & Ball. This is further echoed in the white table and white mount in the artwork. A very clean finish.

The colours below are chosen to show how a cool and a warm palette can work just as well with a shade such as Plum.

Clever combinations with Wild Plum:

| Wild Plum | Ming Gold | | Wild Plum | Bonton |
| Barely Beige | Moonsprite | | Delicacy | Crystal Grey |

ROOM COLOUR

PURPLE

Purple is a very vibrant shade. And true purple is not too light nor not too dark.

Quite unusually you see it here in a master bathroom. With wood and ceramic basins this works because it's neither too masculine nor too feminine.

All White has been used on the ceiling to match in with the pure white tiles.

Purple is underused in residential properties but is used widely in grand homes due to its links with Royalty. It's not a subtle colour but used correctly and minimally, it can make an interior quite special. For maximum effect - go bright!

Clever combinations with Marvellous Purple:

| Marvellous Purple | Drummond | | Marvellous Purple | Ringwold Ground |
| Slaked Lime Dark | French Grey Pale | | Hay | White Tie |

www.homeconscious.com

ROOM COLOUR

LAVENDER

Whisper by Little Greene is the very lightest of purples, but without the grey of Farrow & Ball's Peignoir. It works equally well in a hallway or cloakroom as it does in bedroom, seen here. This owner has really layered on the tones by using creams, whites and lilacs to heighten the sugary effect. This look isn't for everybody but again, colour is a mood giver and changer.

Think about to whom the room belongs and how they will feel when spending any amount of time within it. Darker furniture will make this shade more mature; light furniture as seen here evokes girlish femininity.

Clever combinations with Whisper:

| Whisper | Brinjal | | Whisper | Pale Powder |
| Archive | Dimity | | Hardwick White | Pointing |

ROOM COLOUR

DAMSON

Altogether more sludgy, Light Peachblossom is a shade that is somewhere between taupe and purple, which gives it its muddy appearance. Damson tones need other colours to guide the way. Notably blue and green shades and tints to freshen the Damson tones and richer creams and mushrooms to bring out the purple undertones.

Use Damson in areas that get little sunlight – utility rooms, cloakrooms and passageways. Warm woods also work well with Damson. So use Mahogany, Beech and Walnut with Damson as a backdrop.

The pale blue used to with it here is a popular choice for Damson; purple and blue both sitting in the cooler end of the colour spectrum.

Clever combinations with Light Peachblossom:

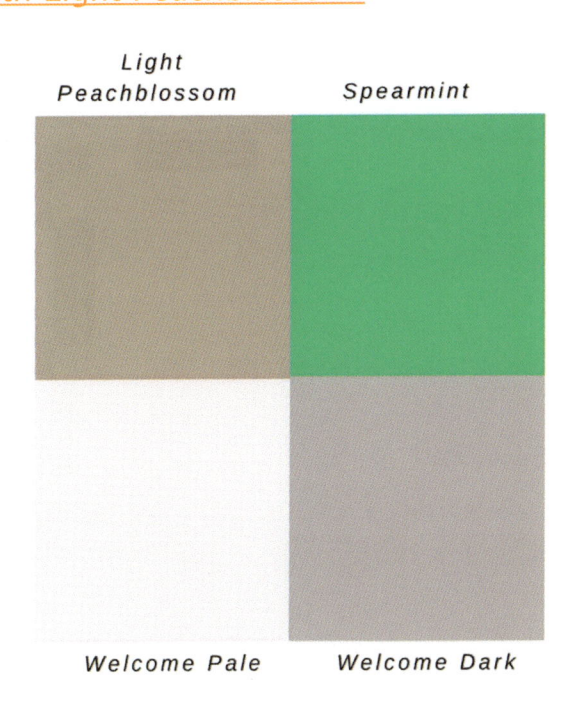

Light Peachblossom	Echo
Orangerie	Hammock

Light Peachblossom	Spearmint
Welcome Pale	Welcome Dark

www.homeconscious.com

GREY

The most used neutral of the last decade, Grey has so many permutations that paint houses have provided special brochures of grey palettes to help you decide what shade is right for your scheme. Everyone uses it and you'll see it in every magazine and every house that you look at. It's inoffensive, modern and practical. In fact, it's hard to avoid. But used carefully and uniquely, you can create something quite special with it that you won't find anywhere else.

The trick is not to over do it when creating a scheme. Men love grey because it's masculine and doesn't make a statement. But painting the whole house grey is a little too copycat - particularly of all those magazine articles.

'USE YOUR GREY MATTER'

What should I avoid putting with Grey?

Dark Brown – one dark neutral is enough!

Black – because Black is the next stage down from Grey, it's advisable to keep these two apart. They also are very reminiscent of 1980s décor, especially if teamed with red!

Where to try it:

Master Bedroom - you can afford to be more appeasing in this room because the colour of these walls should appeal to both sexes. Given that grey can be very calming, it's also ideal for a bedroom.

Top Tip:

Brighten with acid colours of lemon, lime, orange and magenta if you want to add a little more youth to your scheme - rather than mature colours such as burgundy, navy and ivy green.

ROOM COLOUR

LEAD/DARK GREY

Obsidian Green by Little Greene, seen here, is actually an off black but being so close to grey, it's wise to include it here if you are looking for a deep grey.

You may notice that the two beams on the ceiling are a slightly different to the walls. This colour is Knightsbridge by Little Greene. It's a warmer grey than their other deep grey, Dark Lead Colour, and gives just enough difference to the beams in this scheme.

Apart from the combinations below – I've successfully paired Dark Grey with Mustard Yellow! Which proves that Dark Grey is a sophisticated colour that is a good backdrop for any strong colours that you may want to use.

Clever combinations with Dark Lead Colour:

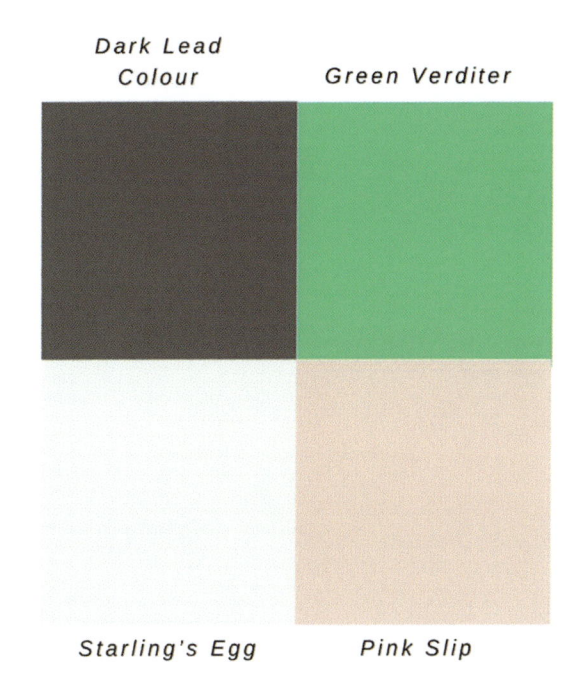

Dark Lead Colour	Orange Aurora		Dark Lead Colour	Green Verditer
Joanna	Rusling		Starling's Egg	Pink Slip

www.homeconscious.com

69

ROOM COLOUR

GUNMETAL

Gunmetal is a silver shade that is mid range on the Grey chart. Close to stainless steel and Pewter, Gunmetal is a metallic shade that has hidden depths. I don't mean it appears darker – quite the contrary – I just mean that it can appear much lighter, given the right accessories and light source.

Seen here is Grey Teal by Little Greene. This rich colour is a great choice for a staircase and whilst the wooden panelling and skirting look white, it's actually the palest of greys – Wood Ash.

A very popular pairing colour with grey is a 70s shade, Marigold. Many shades of Orange would be suitable but Marigold is bright and uncompromising. Using a low level stripe to bridge the gap between the Grey Teal and the Wood Ash is a clever idea. Get a professional decorator to do this for you!

Clever combinations with Grey Teal:

Grey Teal	Turquoise Blue	Grey Teal	Indian Sand
Drizzle	Linen Wash	Tuscany	Julie's Dream

ROOM COLOUR

PALE GREY/FRENCH GREY

The ubiquitous French Grey has classic and inevitable continental connections. Used universally to convey taste, style and understatement, it's the neutral that will never go out of fashion.

Seen here is more of that subtle use of layering within colours. The main wall is French Grey Dark, the low level panelling is French Grey and the fireplace is French Grey Pale. All by Little Greene.

Using French Grey Pale on the fireplace still allows it to stand out. It's kinder to the eye than white and in period properties, will blend in much more easily than sharper whites.

Clever combinations with French Grey:

French Grey	Mambo		French Grey	Firefly
Echo	China Clay		Spearmint	Whitening

www.homeconscious.com

WHITE

White spaces impress with their simplicity and light. You do have to be careful that your room does not resemble an art gallery though. White is also the colour of self importance for many so don't go overboard with too much of this lightest of colours!

The trick with white rooms is to layer the textures and use white only as a statement where it's needed; not throughout the house. Used too liberally, and you will appear unimaginative and pretentious.

Here we see it in a spacious and modern interior. This is Birch White Lt by Sanderson. Oversized pendant lights, gloss tiles and black accessories give this holiday home a superstar vibe.

Clever combinations with Birch White Lt:

Birch White Lt	Chateau Grey	Birch White Lt	Abbey White
Pale Powder	Cosmic Grey	Beach Tan	Peony Pink

MAKING A SCHEME FLOW

The best and most obvious way to create colour flow from room to room is to carry elements of the room colour into each other. These colour connections can be exact (the same blue on the walls throughout the property), or varied. Varying the colours from room to room by varying the intensity of colour within a room is one way to do it. Another way is to use adjacent colour; so perhaps blues and greens together. Remember - you may not want everything to look the same throughout - in which case, create and be as colourful as you feel!

But if you do want a scheme to 'flow' throughout your property, here are some guidelines about placement to consider..

WHAT colour you choose is a matter of preference and daylight. A colour chart is an indispensable tool for helping you choose these shades, especially if you are using the same paint house for all your colours. But if you want to create continuity, select colours in similar tints or shades.

Choose three to four colours and consider *HOW* you want to see them in the space. What colour will be in the background or featured more prominently? To help you decide, look to existing furnishings for colour inspiration. Pick up colours from fabrics, wooden furniture, artwork, or accessories, and use these same colours in different rooms throughout your home.

Which colours will carry through from one room to the next, and *WHERE* will they appear?

Will you see colours through doorways and upstairs? Consider how you'd like to see these colours transition from room to room. For example, perhaps the main wall colour in one room becomes the ceiling colour in another and a feature wall in a further one. You can also use cushions, lampshades, rugs or window treatments to carry these colours from room to room. Select one or two colours that all your rooms will share.

ROOM COLOUR

To put this in order:

1. Walk through your house and note which spaces you can see from each room. Use a floor plan (a rough sketch is fine) to keep track. Note which rooms are visible to one another. Mark arrows on your floor plan showing a line of vision. Adjoining rooms are part of this, but you may be able to see quite a bit farther — down a hall and into the kitchen, for instance.

2. Once you can see what rooms need to be linked through eyesite (where your arrows are on your plan), start by deciding what colour you want to see the most, in the biggest, most important room. This space will most likely be your living room (or kitchen). Once you have that colour, you use your arrows to tell you where, in the adjoining rooms, you should use it to link the two spaces together. It could be you want to draw the eye to a particular wall. It could be a window or a fireplace. Mark this down on your plan. You now know that your chosen colour should be added to these places in each room, in order to create continuity. The alternative to this is starting with the room you want to paint the <u>boldest</u> colour. If you love colour and have a certain colour in mind for a specific room, you can start there. When much of the house is visible at once, as in an open plan space; picking colours that work together is especially important.

3. Work on upstairs and downstairs spaces separately. If there is obvious separation between floors, you can easily create a different mood in the upstairs vs downstairs, defined by the colours you choose. Focusing on one floor at a time can help keep the task manageable!

ROOM COLOUR

THINGS TO REMEMBER WHEN CHOOSING YOUR SCHEME...

- Don't get side-tracked by the name of a colour. These days, Magnolia will put off anyone that lived through the 70's and 80's. So will the term Avocado, given that it was used extensively for bathrooms in the 70's. Paint companies, such as Farrow & Ball or Fired Earth use inventive names for colours that can be contradictory. Little Greene has a colour called Yellow-Pink. It's bright golden yellow to look at but the word pink may well put some people off as well as seeming slightly misleading. If you have colour samples on paper or card with the names written on the reverse, get into the habit of not turning them over to inspect the name. Deal with the colour your eyes are seeing first, not what its name is.

- Colour changes on different materials. So, a Crimson fabric will look darker than a Crimson Perspex table. Paint has far more subtle changes so there is less to worry about. Yes, gloss will appear more vibrant than eggshell which in turn, will appear more vibrant than flat matt emulsion. Texture is good – so don't get too hung up on the same shades looking slightly different on different materials. Exact matches are fun - but they are not imperative.

- Look at paint colours in different lights – morning, afternoon and evening. In daylight and with electric light sources.

- Remember that paint colours can always be made up if you can't find the exact shade you want. Most decorators can do this for you onsite. To be honest, there is such a wealth of colours it will be hard for you not to find something that you like!

- Don't lift your scheme from a magazine. It's good to have those tear sheets and clippings as a guide, but your room will look very different so don't get hung up on what you see in fashionable magazines. Those magazines are meant to sell you things first and foremost and each room has been cleaned, decluttered, expertly styled and professionally photographed – in effect, not lived in. Don't get disheartened by those very polished room sets. Look at contrast and juxtaposition in your scheme. Neutrals can be simple but adding contrast on your walls with colour can demonstrate your creativity in a bolder way. If you make a mistake – please do not worry. It is only paint and can be painted over very simply.

Let's now get started with organising and choosing your scheme..

YOUR PROJECT – YOUR SCHEME

Colour Cards

There are various paint houses and they all produce colour cards. To save you the time of going to all the main ones individually, Designer Paint has put them all together. Here's the link so you can get them sent out to you.

http://www.designerpaint.com /pages/colour-folio.php

There are obviously more paint houses – but those are the main ones that I mainly use.

GUIDE SHEETS

Your room, your choice..

Armed with your Guide Sheet and Worksheets (if you have purchased those) grab your Paint Colour Cards and sit somewhere quiet and comfortable.

If you have arrived via Amazon, you can upgrade and grab your worksheets and guide sheets here:

Guide Sheets, Worksheets and Idea Sheets Link

Have fun! How about working up 3 schemes and choosing the best one at the end?

Let's get started..

Assessment

The first stage is Assessment. You need to understand your room, the light, the proportions, what the room will be used for and what furniture needs to go in the room. This is so you can build your scheme from the ground up.

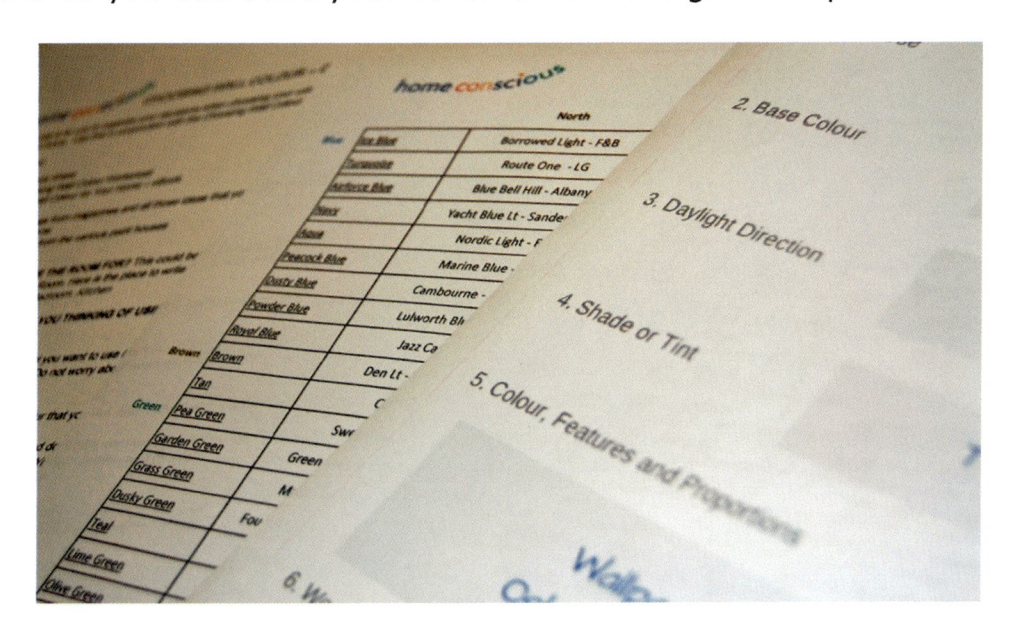

STEP 1

WHAT WILL YOU USE THE ROOM FOR?

I only ask this as there can sometimes be a change of use for a room when people renovate. What once was a bedroom, now becomes a Study. A Dining Room becomes a TV Den for teenagers. You need to clarify how you're going to use the room going forward.

Once you know its use, you can move onto suitable colours for that specific room. There is no hard and fast rule for what colour must be used for a particular room, but it is well to keep in mind the mood you are trying to create. Have a think about what colour is right for the purpose of that room.

Let's look at this in a bit more detail:

- Bedrooms work best in light, relaxing colours. But don't be bound by this. If you want to go dark and moody, do!

- Dining Rooms tend to be formal and bold and can handle Ivy Green, Crimson, Aubergine and Amber if you would like a grand effect.

- Living Rooms are the most interesting to choose as they have to accommodate various activities and are the 'show piece' of the property – you can afford to be bold and surprising. Teal, Golden Yellow, Navy and Chocolate are always very popular.

- Bathrooms tend to be painted in Blue due to the link with water. But consider other colours to be different. Bathrooms often have very little light, sometimes no natural light at all, so keeping to a lighter shade can be best for rooms of a limited size. Contemplate Lemon, Peach or Mint to inject something different into the smallest room. Pick your tiles first and then your paint colour afterwards!

- Children's Rooms are usually and sadly either Blue or Pink. I never use these colours for children's rooms unless I am specifically asked to do so. I look at Lilac, Butterscotch, Peach, Mint and Aqua.

ROOM COLOUR

- Kitchens are the anomaly. Because kitchen units are often from stock and are pre-coloured, you will need to work with those colours. Most are Brilliant White. Many are natural wood and some are a veneer (a thin layer of wood applied over particle boards or panels). Others are deep colours in gloss. Get a sample from your kitchen supplier to help you decide what shade to go with.

- Other rooms such as Studies are often painted Grey and Conservatories end up Green. There are less of these rooms, so come with far less stereotypical baggage these days!

STEP 2

WHAT COLOUR BASE ARE YOU THINKING OF USING?

Once you know what the room is going to be used for, the next step is to choose what type of atmosphere you envisage from this room. And from this you can choose your base colour (eg: yellow, blue, pink, cream).

There are a number of ways to start this process. You might want a fresh feel, or you might want something cosy yet grand or maybe you want something quiet and mellow.

Sometimes you may have a fabric that you want to base a scheme on and that fabric is folksy Yellow or perhaps plush Crimson. Or you just really want a Powder Blue bedroom because it's soft yet fresh. Either way, the base colour is the thing to decide upon at this point. It doesn't matter if this changes as you can work up several schemes with different base colours, the important thing is to start with one.

It is at this stage that you need to look at your inspiration notes and tear sheets if you have them. Specifically, you want those tear sheets that relate to the specific room you are going to design.

What is a 'tear sheet'?

This is a magazine page torn from a magazine that you have kept because you liked a colour, a style, a piece of furniture, a floor lamp, a cushion or something else that you loved when you saw it. These are, in essence, Mood Boards or Files. They centralise and organise your aspirations and ideas for your home.

ROOM COLOUR

An online alternative to this is something like Pinterest. This has as many boards as you want and the ability for you to take photos and add them to your Mood Board digitally. Well worth it getting a (free) account for. I tend to organise mine into 'inspiration' boards (I have millinery, stylish movies and even the Duchess of Windsor as boards!) and then I have more specific boards of themes (aquatic, black and white and Riviera) to organise looks. I don't use them all the time. But I do use them from time to time and I encourage my clients to create versions of their own.

Another tool to use is Apple's Shared Photos. This enables you to share photos or tear sheets with your family or interior designer - to let them know the direction of things to take.

These Pinterest boards or Shared Photo Albums will help organise your thoughts and visuals in a way that mood boards used to. Mood Boards are still used in many industries. Essentially these are boards of about A3 size or maybe 2ft square and have a blank canvas. You then pin, glue or hang various inspirational items onto the boards to create a collection of colour, texture and mood for your chosen project. Texture is the most important item in a moodboard and something that Shared Albums and Pinterest can't really compete with - being as they are, digital.

For our purposes, colour is able to be shown fairly accurately in digital form (though the paint houses will disagree with this!) so Pinterest and Shared Photo Albums are adequate for our use.

I would suggest getting yourself a Pinterest account, if you don't already have one, and starting a board for each room of your property. Then you can move 'pins' from one board to another as you progress your scheme.

Make sure you cover all aspects of your paint scheme - feature walls, textures and very importantly, woodwork.

STEP 3

WORKING WITH DAYLIGHT AND COLOUR - WHICH DIRECTION IS YOUR ROOM FACING?

The next thing to ascertain is which direction the room faces. If you don't have a compass handy (who does these days?!) use the compass on your smartphone. Often, a colour which looked great in a friend's house in a sunny south-facing room, doesn't work when you try it in a north-facing room on a grey winter's day in your own house.

How Daylight Affects Colours

As the amount and angle of the sun changes, so will your room colours. Natural light should always be considered when choosing colour for a space. Most paint companies are good at explaining which neutrals are "warm or cold" tinted, so "red", "yellow" or "grey" based etc. and this is a good basic guide to getting things right, although the advice can be confusing. Let's look at the different aspects of each facing room...

North-Facing Rooms:

Northern light is a cool, pure, blue-toned light that can make a room appear cold. It is the 'truest light'. Service spaces, such as utilities and bathrooms, are frequently positioned to the north with smaller windows, to prevent the areas from becoming warm. Due to the coolness, North-facing rooms can be notoriously difficult to decorate because they receive the least natural light throughout the day. So bolder colours show up better than muted colours and lighter colours look subdued or grey.

What to go for: Embrace what nature has supplied. I would recommend using a strong dark colour — purples, leafy greens, deep blues, tobacco, sand and chocolates which will create both intimacy and drama. However, if you prefer lighter tones, choose a neutral with a creamy or yellow base. Taupe works well, but steer clear of any grey or cool undertones as these will make the room feel colder still.

ROOM COLOUR

South-Facing Rooms:

Usually, people associate south-facing windows with enjoying the best natural (warm-toned) light. In response, many house builders locate their main living rooms to the south, specifying larger windows to increase the sun's rays. So, these are the easiest rooms to decorate, as they get the best light throughout the day.

Lots of high level light brings out the best in cool and warm colours. Dark colours will look brighter; lighter colours will pleasingly glow. Tone-wise, both warm and cool colours will look good, and you're free to choose what sort of atmosphere you want to encourage in the room, although remember colours will be intensified in the sun.

What to go for: Pale colours will give the room a feeling of light and space. You could use pale cool blues if you want to create a fresh feel. For a warm and sophisticated feel, use a red based neutral colour. Yellow also works extremely well and will highlight the sunny nature of these rooms.

TOP TIP: Avoid building conservatories or garden rooms with glass roofs facing south, as these will overheat and are better located to the east or west.

East-Facing Rooms:

East light is warm and yellowy before noon, then turns cooler and bluer later in the day. These are great rooms for reds, oranges and yellows. East-facing rooms are bright as they get the morning sun light but by evening, rooms will have changed dramatically resulting in shadows and becoming blue-tinged.

Bedrooms that face east will be cooler in the late afternoon and evening, making them more comfortable for summer sleeping. Early risers generally appreciate east sun in spaces they will use first thing in the morning, such as kitchens.

What to go for: Pale duck egg colours (and those with tones of green) will sing first thing but will retain warmth for the evening sunset. Consider a blue colour scheme for this room – why fight nature? Use eggshell or gloss on your woodwork to add more light and texture in the shadows.

TOP TIP: Add in additional light sources for an east facing room – floor and table lamps will ensure the room remains 'warm'.

West-Facing Rooms:

West facing rooms are quite dark in the morning with scant morning light producing shadows, making colours look dull. They have good afternoon daylight though and evening light in these rooms is beautiful and warm. As west-facing rooms get low-angle, late afternoon sun, they usually require some shading to prevent overheating and excessive glare, particularly during the summer. A west-facing orientation is suitable as a living area in households where occupants are away from home during the day-time but at home in the evenings. It is not generally suitable as a kitchen as the heat from dinner preparation coincides with low-angled afternoon and evening sun, potentially causing glare and overheating.

What to go for: Evening sun, which west-facing rooms get the most of, works well with pink, red and orange tones, while off white is a natural light reflector and can bounce around the room magnificently, enhancing both natural and artificial light. A soft pink or peach can be a perfect compromise between the two, creating a warm glow without losing too much of the light.

Maximising Natural Daylight

To make the most of the natural light that enters a room, we must create surfaces in our rooms that are highly reflective. One of the most effective ways to spring natural light around a room is to ensure the room is furnished in the brightest colours you are willing to have in the space.

Another great way to add an additional reflective surface is the use of a large mirror on your wall. By finding a sleek, stylish mirror that fits well with the theme in your room, you can make the natural light you have go even further, and add a great new feature too.

By ensuring some of the larger features in your room such as sofas, dining tables or desks are light in colour too, you can maximise a room potential when it comes to sharing the light. When choosing furnishings, remember that white and pale colours will reflect the light, while warm colours will absorb it. To maximize light within fabrics use material with metallic accents, such as linens with silver weaves, to create highlights within the space.

STEP 4

DO YOU HAVE AN EXACT SHADE OR TINT IN MIND?

Simply choosing 'blue' as a colour for your room won't be enough. There are thousands of them. So you'll need to choose a particular shade/tint and that can be daunting as well as exciting. Inspiration comes from many places. Tear sheets are invaluable here. Looking at these can really help you decide what shade would be right for you long term.

Nevertheless, you should ask yourself important questions. Can you see yourself living in that colour room long term? Will you get bored? Is it practical? Importantly, is there a colour that is coming up frequently in your tear sheets? Be honest! Is it the style in the photo or the colour that you like? Once you have explored all the options, it's here that you marry the two elements of base colour and daylight to choose your shade for the walls of your room or at least, 3 out of the 4 walls of the room. Use the guidelines in Step 3 to narrow down your choice from 'blue' to 'navy blue' or from 'pink' to 'cerise pink'. Don't worry about exact paint colour names at this point.

STEP 5

FEATURES, HIGHLIGHTS, ISSUES, PROPORTIONS

Colour in daylight and its effects are fairly well known. What is less well known is the effect of colour on room proportion. Colour is very powerful and, if used correctly, can alter proportions quite dramatically. Making rooms appear wider or longer can all be done with colour. It is for this reason that you should remember these key attributes of cooler and warmer shades when deciding on feature walls – if you are going to have any that is.

If your room is very narrow or overwhelmingly large, deciding on a colour to help draw the eye could be key.

Colours fall into either 'Receding' or 'Advancing' categories. Colours that **'recede away'** are:
- Blue
- Green
- Purple (light shades such as Lilac or Lavender in particular)
- Grey

Colours that **'advance towards'** are:
- Red
- Yellow
- Orange
- Pink

You will notice that it is the cool colours that recede away and the warm colours that advance towards you. So, if you have a narrow room, then choosing a soft peach colour for the wall that is furthest away will make the room appear more square. Likewise, a cool blue on a protruding chimney breast will make it sink into the supporting walls. It is partly for this reason that 'feature walls' have become so prevalent in recent decades. People like symmetry and the illusion of a well balanced room.

So, there are ways to change the illusion of proportions in a room. But there are a few other different effects that you can try, if you want to be a little more inventive with colour. These could have a bearing on your choice of colour, so it's important that you consider these before making any definite decisions.

Not all will be right for you or your property and for commercial properties, it is wise to get someone experienced to do your decorating – especially if you are going to try something avant garde. But if you are at home, and most of you are, then take a look at the following options you have to inject something a little different into your scheme.

FEATURE WALLS

Feature walls – the process of painting one or sometimes two walls in a different colour to the majority of walls is not a new concept. But it has been used by those who are not courageous enough to add a room full of colour. This usually manifests as one 'bright bold wall' and the rest in a 'calm neutral'.

An alternative to this would be a feature wall in wallpaper – but more on wallpaper in another book!

This is called an 'ombre' effect and is usually found in fabrics rather than in wall finishes. Used by those who want to make a statement and those who are both brave and creative in equal measure, it is an effect that demands unfettered access to walls with little or no wall art. Notice how the furniture is set away from the wall and how they have restricted the palette to maximise the impact of the blue.

ROOM COLOUR

Here two paint colours are used to create a Dado effect around the room. Many period properties had these Dado rails (used to protect walls from the backs of chairs) and most have been removed – creating a practical need for this kind of detail with paint. The upper part of these walls are Lead White with the lower part of the wall is Stone Dark Cool. The woodwork has been finished in Lead White to blend seamlessly in with the upper wall. All colours by Little Greene.

ROOM COLOUR

A steady hand or stencilling is used to create this stripey effect.

Wall: (Top to Bottom) Whitening; Canton; Turquoise Blue ; Baked Cherry; Whitening; Canton; Green Verditer; Whitening; Turquoise Blue; Baked Cherry; Whitening; Canton.

All these colours are used in a kaleidoscope effect that effectively becomes artwork for the wall. When you make a decision to implement this type of wall design you must ensure that your furniture, lighting and accessories are kept simple and minimal. Do not try to add competing elements – leave the paint work to take centre stage.

ROOM COLOUR

A really interesting design here on the right with Fired Earth paints. *Clockwise:* Orchard Pink, Graphite, Skylon Grey, Yes Your Honour and Storm.

This type of design takes time to map out and to really think about what the end result will be. Because extra time will be needed, both for planning, mapping and executing, speak to your decorator so that he can factor the time necessary into your decorating schedule.

On your worksheet/paper, note if you plan to add in a feature wall to your room and what effect you would like it to have. This part is optional.

STEP 6

WOODWORK CHOICES

WOODWORK

Painting woodwork is somewhere that you can be a little different.

Most woodwork that you will see in both domestic and commercial properties will be White. The reason for this is overwhelmingly habit, secondly it is cost and thirdly, lack of effort. White or Off-White is used as it is the most basic neutral and will tend to match in most colours. Using a different colour on the woodwork shows flair, adds interest and can be useful against wear and tear.

Don't think that you have to go with white on woodwork. Using a colour on woodwork was traditionally seen as old fashioned but not anymore. Frequently used in Victorian interiors, darker woodwork was painted to tie in with mahogany furniture, banisters and flooring. Today, darker woodwork is used to add drama and practicality. I've often used darker woodwork in hallways – knowing how much traffic they get and how woodwork can get knocked in passageways. Dust and dirt also accumulates in hallways so a darker shade on the skirtings can be a blessing.

Brighter woodwork can often be a scene stealer and should be used carefully and sparingly. They will highlight the very items that are painted, drawing your eye to them. You have four choices:

1. Use the expected neutral of White or Off White
2. Use a different neutral such as Taupe or Grey
3. Use a colour to either complement or contrast
4. Use the same colour as the walls

ROOM COLOUR

Here below, they have used Option A. They have used two Little Greene colours; Attic II on the walls with a stripe bordering the skirting and architrave in Sky Blue. It may not sound the most inviting name but Attic II gives a striking effect with the bright blue. The woodwork in Shirting sharpens the eye and provides the ultimate contrast to the walls.

Notice how the flooring has been kept dark and no attempt has been made to add any further colour to this scheme. It's as well to note that this is an unusual combination and needs thought and care with a view to existing furniture, curtains and flooring if you are going to implement this scheme.

ROOM COLOUR

Below is Option B. The woodwork is a neutral. Calming, practical and easy on the eye, this kitchen unit could be painted to match the kitchen units that surround the rest of the kitchen, or be painted to stand out and complement. In this case, the idea is to blend. The woodwork is painted the same as the skirting and door frame.

ROOM COLOUR

Below is Option C. The bright coral pink of this door has been chosen to stand out against the grey of the walls. Door panelling can be lost when painted white or cream, but using a brighter colour can make a simple door seem almost artisan. To further differentiate the separate parts and to increase the 'artwork' illusion, a brilliant white architrave surrounds the pink. Notice how the door ironmongery is polished brass – not the usual brushed steel. This draws the eye and increases the decorative effect.

On your worksheet/paper, write down whether you want a lighter or darker shade of woodwork. Again, don't worry about exact paint colour names right now. Also, add any additional woodwork ideas you have onto your worksheet.

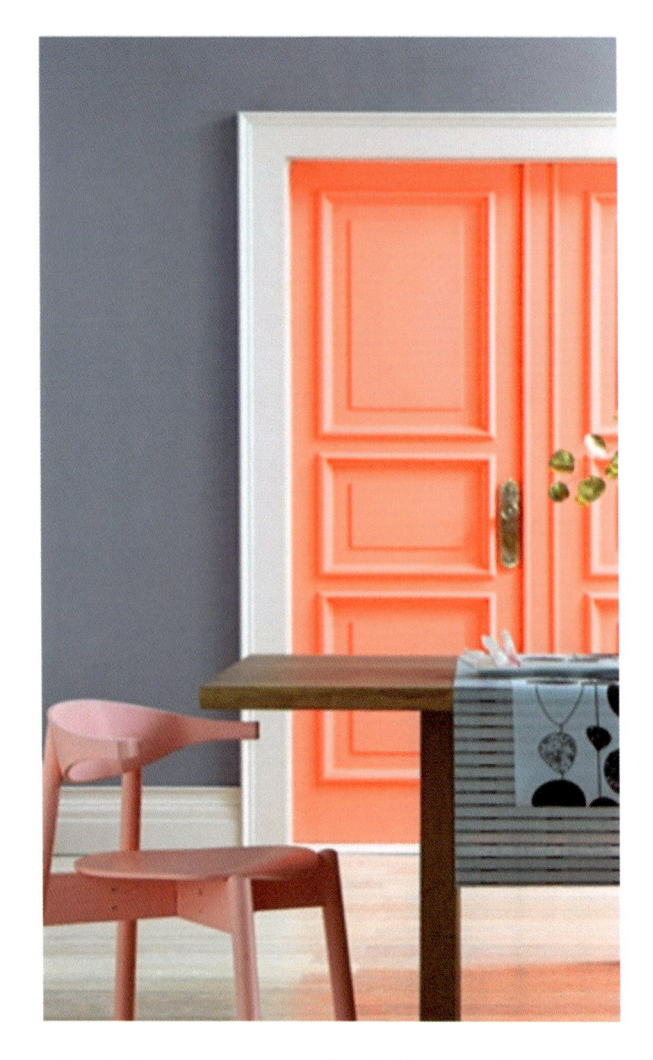

Top Tip!—If you are looking to use bright paintwork in children's rooms then make sure you paint the inside of the children's door in the bright shade and leave the hallway side in the shade of the hallway paintwork

RADIATORS

There is one rule that I live by with radiators. If I can paint them to blend in with the wall, then I do. There is nothing more annoying to a colour scheme than a stainless steel or brilliant white radiator 'standing out'. Your decorator may have to use a special paint to withstand the heat of your radiator, but it is necessary! Below we see a blend of Little Greene's. The wall is in Stock, the architrave and panel behind is in Stock Deep and the radiator itself is in Stock Dark.

CEILINGS

Often called the fifth wall, ceilings are often overlooked, but painting them a specific colour can really bring a room to life. But is it ever wise to paint the ceiling anything other than White? The short answer is yes. Whilst it is not always wise to go with a bold colour in small rooms or rooms with a low ceiling, adding colour from above can produce a great effect. But you don't have to go bright or even a medium hued shade.

Below: The owner of this spare bedroom has chosen a Fuchsia Pink to enliven this room. Whilst the walls and woodwork remain neutral, the ceiling brightens the scheme and is echoed in the headboards, poof and bedspreads.

ROOM COLOUR

Here are some tips when painting ceilings:

1. The Most Popular Choice - white paint makes ceilings appear higher and brighter than they actually are. When the walls are white too, the room is airy and open, but can look too stark. Be wary of using 'bright white' on both walls and ceilings. Even though using white paint on the ceiling is the most popular choice! The good news is that as the paint ages on the walls and softens; so will the ceiling paint. So it won't always look so 'bright' and 'new'.

2. To Gain Height In A Room - try using a sympathetic white for the ceiling. That is, when you're using colour on the wall, go for a ceiling colour that has tints of the wall colour. So you're less aware of where walls end and ceilings begin.

3. To Make A High Ceiling Appear Lower - choose deeper and warmer off-whites. And to make it seem higher choose a more definite white like the Brilliant white that most decorators use.

4. For A Cosier Feel - a slightly darker shade on the ceiling than the walls will make the ceiling feel lower and more intimate. This is perfect for a bedroom or bathroom where you want to relax and linger. Think about going down this route if your ceilings are really tall, so it doesn't feel like the room is closing in on you.

5. Adding A Soft Blush To A Room - by painting a pale cream or a soft pink to the ceiling, you can add a soft blush to a room and can blossom an overall effect.

6. Consider The Cornice or Picture Rail - If you do choose to add colour to the ceiling, you will have to consider the cornice, if you have one. To paint with the walls or with the ceiling? Don't be afraid to take the paint colour of the walls all the way up over the picture rail. This will add height to the walls.

STEP 7

ASSESSING YOUR FURNITURE AND ACCESSORIES

Most people will have furniture or accessories that they need to work around. Whether this is a sofa, a pair of curtains, a rug or a chest of drawers, it doesn't matter. The important thing is to recognise that you have something that your colour scheme will work alongside.

- Sofa – for such a large item, it's worth looking at whether it is being kept and if so, whether it is being recovered/re-upholstered. Whilst this may be an added expense, it would be a good time to do this as the item will be taken away and will be out of the way during the decoration phase.

- Rug – again, is it being kept and if so, now would be a good time to get it cleaned. Preferably off site – due to the dust during decorating. Patterned rugs can be more forgiving than block colours.

- Curtains – these are something that will need to be worked into your scheme if they are staying. Your eye will naturally be drawn to any window so curtains and blinds must fit into your colour scheme. It could be that you replace your current curtains with a sharper Roman blind as a blind will be tidier and will be less material than curtains will be.

- Furniture – if you have items that are natural wood then, it may make sense for all woods to match in order to make your scheme more coherent. Using different woods in one room can be jarring on specific colour schemes so keep woods together, whether they are mahogany, oak, teak or pine. If it is preferable to paint the odd item (and add new handles for example) then now would also be a good time to do this.

- Bed and Headboard – whilst beds are not in every room and may not carry any colour as such, it is wise to consider them when designing your colour scheme. Wooden or iron bedsteads will need different considerations than upholstered divans. Re-upholstering can be expensive for an entire bed but recovering a headboard can be very cost effective and worth doing to add a colour and/or texture into a scheme.

- Lamps – these are easier to replace if necessary and often just a change of shade will suffice when updating your scheme. I often change lamps around in the home. It can effectively change things up without any cost except your time.

- Cushions and Throws – probably the easiest thing to change and definitely the cheapest way to update any interior colour scheme. Whether its cushions on your bed or your sofa or on a bench in your kitchen diner, cushions are small patches of colour that can be taken away or changed at will. I love variety so often change mine every season; both for cleaning and aesthetic reasons. Throws are more a recent invention used for both decorative and comfort purposes. It's best that your cushions and throws work together as they will often be seen together on larger items of furniture.

The important thing with accessories is that if you have something you love, the chances are that you will always love it. I never throw cushion covers, throws, table lamps or rugs away if I am bored with them. I store them (either in the loft or off site) and come back to them with a fresh eye, many months later. Make sure they are stored clean and repaired. If you are still bored with them after a year or the next time you see them, feel free to sell or donate them. But take your time and don't make rash decisions. Schemes change and you may have use for them in another part of your home.

Summarising Your Information

You should now know:

- What room you are going to decorate
- Your ideal base colour
- What natural light source your room depends on; which direction
- What specific shade you would like to choose from
- Optional - whether you are adding feature walls into the room and what proportional ideas you have for them
- What woodwork idea (light or dark) you would like to choose from
- What current and existing items you need to incorporate into your scheme with their base colours

STEP 8

CHOOSING SPECIFIC SHADES

Your final steps are to choose a wall colour and a woodwork colour that fits in with your plan.

You can either leaf through your paint charts and look at your chosen tone (dusky blue, golden yellow etc) and decide which one to go for or try, OR you can grab my Daylight and Colour Shades Ideas Chart, as I've done all the work for you!

Look along the top for the daylight direction and then down the chart until you reach your chosen shade. It would be a good idea to try sampling the colours either side of your main option to give yourself something to compare to. On the worksheet/paper, write down your options.

Do the same when it comes to the woodwork shade. Grab my Woodwork Ideas sheet and look at the ideas for a lighter woodwork or a darker woodwork. Write these down so your worksheet is complete.

Sampling with real paint

When you have decided on your paint or paints to try, your final stage is to check them on the walls of the room that they are destined for.

ROOM COLOUR

Some designers put paint onto large pieces of cardboard or paper and move them from room to room. I always think this is a mistake. Your walls do not move and are not made of paper and cardboard! It's an old method that confuses many when it's tried. The only time this is ever prudent to do is when you have clients that are entertaining in the property and it would look messy to apply paint swatches to the walls. But even then, you can usually find some hidden place to start the proper sampling (look behind doors and curtains!).

How to sample:

- Put down newspaper/plastic/anything protective onto the floor beneath the wall you are applying paint to - you will get drips!
- Keep some kitchen towel or toilet roll handy for spills and drips if you just starting this work
- Keep the tops of sample pots with their bottom halves for ease - and rest these on paper too
- Choose the wall that is neither in shade nor in direct sunlight - you want a balanced view
- Put your paint 'squares' direct onto the wall.
- I always use make up sponges to apply them rather than paint as they are easy to wash or indeed throw away after usage.
- Make sure your paint squares are at least 20cm by 20cm in size; ideally 30cm by 30cm
- Do not put them too close to the next sample square or your eye will be confused.
- Apply two coats for proper coverage of the square, letting the first coat dry before applying the second
- Write the name of the colour paint (in pencil!) underneath the squares as you go - do NOT leave it until you have finished painting or you will forget which square is which!

So that's all you need to know and do. I hope this has been of some help to you (and your clients!). I've answered some Frequently Asked Questions below with regards to decorating in general as these are things that come up time and time again. Let me know if you need anything else answered in the course of your interior decoration!

ROOM COLOUR

Frequently Asked Questions:

A few questions that I get asked on a daily basis..

1. Why does a small bathroom cost as much as an average sized sitting room to paint?

   This is due to 'cutting in' or, in plain speak, all the painting around the various pipes, panels, tiles and switches in a bathroom. Getting behind a toilet or a sink, takes extra time - or at least the same amount of time to roller a large empty wall. It's the detailed work that takes the time - often whilst protecting built in furniture and suites - that makes bathrooms (and kitchens for that matter) the same price as larger rooms.

2. What's the difference between satin wood, eggshell and gloss?

   Eggshell is the most popular these days, as it has an almost matt finish and blends in well with emulsion walls. It's the subtle, softer look for woodwork. Most spray painted joinery is in eggshell for a very sophisticated look

   Slightly shinier is **Satin Wood** - this is more durable and practical and is often used in children's rooms. Use this for bathrooms, hallways, kitchens and nurseries.

   Top for durability is **Gloss**. Used for high traffic areas (particularly hallways) it can take knocks from children, toys, shopping and bicycles whilst giving a polished look to any interior.

3. What type of paint should I use for my bathroom if there is no ventilation?

   In most parts of the house, emulsion is the paint that is used. Emulsion comes in a range of different finishes such as matt and silk as well as variations in-between such as eggshell, soft sheen or satin. Matt emulsion has a non-reflective appearance and is great for uneven walls while silk creates a shiny finish and is great for high use areas such as halls, staircases as well as for kids' bedrooms. You can also get one-coat emulsion that needs a single coat to cover the walls as it is thicker than normal paint.

   Bathroom paint is a specialist type of emulsion that is designed to withstand the moisture levels in a bathroom and also to help prevent mould. This is a common problem in bathrooms, especially if the room doesn't have the right amount of ventilation. Bathroom paints tend to be scrub resistant and have a mid-level of sheen. Typically, they take around 1-2 hours to dry.

The most common problem that I see with regards to bathroom paint, involve the use of a normal paint in the bathroom and a lack of ventilation. This can create mould and spores. While mould spores are a real problem, they aren't an incurable one. The solution is to scrub down the areas affected by the mould to ensure that all of the spores are gone. A water and bleach mix is the best thing to use for this. Once the black patches are gone, leave the area to dry for a good few hours.

Once it is dry, then the room is ready for painting with proper bathroom paint. The anti-mould element in the paint will prevent the spores from accumulating again in the future, though good ventilation is always recommended. Even if this means leaving a window open a small amount, this air flow combined with the right bathroom paint will make for a mould-free room in the future.

4. Can water damage be painted over easily?

Water damage to a property is common - especially with the amount of flats and apartments that there now are. Water damage is more so in the winter period, when the weather is coldest and it is more likely then that frozen water, expanding in the pipes, can cause ruptures and breaks. There are fewer things more unsightly on a pristine white painted ceiling than the glaring splodge of creeping brown damp. The brown stains that are so often the first sign of a leaking pipe from the room above are caused by the minerals within the water which soak through the decor. The water itself can dry out if there is a free air flow over the damaged area, but the unsightly stain will remain unless it is painted over in the right way. Water stains will often bleed through new paint layers if they are not treated correctly in the first instance. The foremost thing, and the most obvious, is to stop the source of the leak itself. Once the leak is stopped, and any repair work carried out, it is important to let the damp area dry out thoroughly. Once it is completely dry, then the first job is to prime the surface with a damp seal product. Often, this will need more than one coat to try and be sure the stain won't bleed through onto the new paint. When the primer is dry and the seal is secure, then the painting and decorating work can begin.

5. What is an undercoat? (not to be confused with an undertone!)

   Often called a primer or a sealer, an undercoat is something that is not really needed if your wall is in good condition (no chunks of plaster missing!) with no flaky patches. With the modern paints we have in this century, undercoating is mostly not necessary.

   If you are worried about existing paint showing through your new paint, you may well decide to paint three coats (instead of the usual two) to ensure the colour is as true as you want and coverage is complete.

   Undercoats are not the same as damp sealant paint (see question 4 above).

   If you are painting **new woodwork**, you can paint over timber knots with a wood primer, otherwise the sap in them will bleed through subsequent coats of paint causing little bubbles of sap to appear a few months or even a year down the line. Apply wood primer (undercoat) followed by your chosen wooden paint. Use an oil-based primer with gloss or eggshell paint.

   MDF. **Unpainted MDF** needs sealing before painting. Use a specialist sealant such as MDF primer, before eggshell, satin wood or gloss.

   If you are painting wood that has been painted previously, no undercoat is required; just wash and sand it.

6. What is 'Cutting In'?

   Cutting In is a decorating term that means to paint the borders and edges of a particular surface. It is the detail work behind pipes, tiles and units in bathroom and kitchens. It's painting in and around cornices, skirtings and picture rails. It also means the work around light fitting recesses and switchplates. Special brushes can and are used to achieve a straight line.

A Few Words of Wisdom

- Please do not worry about getting colour wrong - just try again and get it right for you.

- Don't do half a room - think of the room as a whole and get all elements lined up before starting your project.

- If you are moving into a property for the first time, live in the space for a number of weeks so you can see how the light falls and how you will use each room. This is crucial to do before you start thinking of colours, shades and tints.

- If buying a used property, really work on your visualisation to help you see the possibilities and see PAST what others have done in the space before you.

Remember, it's only paint!
Belinda

THANK YOU

If you have loved this ebook and want more on either this subject or another topic, let me know by emailing belinda@homeconscious.com

I'd love to hear from you on what you would like to learn about next!

I've spent many months compiling this information and content for you. It's taken months of effort to get this far. I would appreciate it if you would respect this and not share or distribute this ebook without my permission. Thank you.

I would like to thank my good friend Izzi for her words of encouragement and help in making this book workable and readable for you all. May she assist me in editing all my future books!

One final thank you must go to Dinishika, my virtual assistant, without whom this book would not have been possible. A very heartfelt thank-you to her!

ABOUT THE AUTHOR

I started my journey many years ago and have learned so much that I think it's about time I shared some knowledge; and give back to those people just starting out on their own journey.

I was never the interior designer when I was young. The only indication was my compulsion, every few months, to move all the furniture around my bedroom to create a different look and a fresh environment. But I was never one to plump up cushions or demand a certain colour paint for my room - that came much later!

Interior Design is not an easy job. It's full of organisation, dedication and detail. I happen to love it - but I know there will be difficult clients, temperamental suppliers and sometimes, late deliveries. You just have to roll with the punches.

If you want to hear about those punches and keep track of my latest projects - sign up for my newsletter at www.homeconscious.com

DISCLAIMER

The printed colours in this book have been matched to each individual colour chart from the relevant paint manufacturer. However, neither the author nor paint house can take any responsibility for any discrepancies in colour between a digital swatch in this book and specified paint from a paint house.

It is important to note that different batches of paint from any manufacturer will vary minutely in colour. When buying paint, always check the batch numbers on the tin (your decorator can advise and help you) and buy from the same batch whenever possible.

PHOTO CREDITS:

Cover -	www.littlegreene.com

Back Cover -	www.littlegreene.com

Pages:	20, 21, 22, 26, 27, 29, 32, 36, 44, 52, 59,
64, 66, 67, 87, 94, 96, 101	www.istockphoto.com

Pages:	38, 45, 47, 48, 49, 50, 53, 60, 61, 65, 72	www.dreamstime.com

Pages:	23, 31, 33, 34, 35, 39, 40, 41, 43, 55, 56 58,
69, 70, 71, 76, 88, 89, 92, 93, 95	www.littlegreene.com

Pages:	25, 57, 63, 90	www.firedearth.com

Authors Own:	30, 77, 80, 109

Page 33 - Aqua

Props: Geo Tray, £22, Future Found. Colander, £36, Future Found. Large Pitcher ivory, £55, Folklore. Medium blue jug, £53, small jug, £25, Duck Egg platter, £197, all from a selection at Mud Australia. Stripe Tea towel, £10, Future Found. Bar Stool

Two, £450, Another Country. Daisy Rug, £130, Northwood Home. Other items all stylist's own.

Page 55 Woodwork - Pea Green

Pedestal table: The Dormy House, Louis Armchair: The Dormy House, White flower pot: Decorative Country living. French wine glasses: Decorative Country Living, Fabric: Jane Churchill.

In foreground: White Wedgwood Jardiniere, Pimpernel & Partners. White bowl, Sophie Conran for Portmeirion. White pot, Decorative Country Living

ROOM COLOUR

Woodwork (brown wall with blue stripe, white frame)

Vintage leather case, from a selection at Pedlars. Hand thrown white vase, £59, Oggetto. White vase from a selection at Oka. Stone bottle, £5, Lost and Found. Glass from a selection at John Lewis. Desk: find similar at The Old Cinema. Lamp: find similar at Skandium. Chair: find similar at Twenty Twenty One

Page 95 Radiator

Sunflowers oil painting: Pimpernel & Partners

Page 34 Peacock Blue

White jars and ceramics from a selection at Brissi, John Lewis, Sainsbury's and Ikea.

Page 71 French Grey

Percy chair: Pimpernel & Partners, Antique mirror: Find similar at Artefact, Hurricane lamps on mantelpiece: Lombok. Antique books on mantle: Artefact. Glass jar on mantle: Designers Guild, Candle votive on mantle: Graham and Green, Butterfly picture: Graham and Green, Task Table Light in Putty Grey: Original BTC, Side table: Pimpernel & Partners, Log basket: Lombok. Lime green toile fabric: Etienne 3597 Harlequin. Cranbury Park Prints LF0827C/002 Wild Mushroom fabric (just seen): Linwood Fabrics. On ottoman: Cream wool throw: Ikea. Candle votive: Graham and Green. Glass vase: Decorative Country Living

Page 93 Kitchen Unit Woodwork

Wallpaper: Lower George St – Beryl £61.00 per roll, Leksand Chair: Scumble Goosie, White jug: Ikea. On shelves: Shoe lasts, Bailey's Home and Garden. Antique books, Artefact. China jug, Pimpernel and Partners. Candle, Ikea. Glass bud vase, Designers Guild. Vintage keys, Re-Found Objects. Cream jug and mug, find similar at Oka.

Page 69 Lead/Dark Grey

Rosewood sideboard, 1970's lamp, and Anglepoise floor lamp, all from a selection at The Old Cinema. Wicker egg chair, find similar at The Old Cinema. Coffee table, find similar at Twenty Twenty One. Picasso framed print, £70, Andy Warhol Green Sam Print, £30, Glass utility vase, £24, Svaja bird paperweight, £20, all John Lewis.

ROOM COLOUR

Cocktail glass, £8, Magnifying glass, £22, both Zara Home. Cushions in 200-73 Poppy, Sandberg ;Stag cushion, £165, Pedlars. Flooring Sisal Malay Tongli £41.50 per sq.m, Alternative Flooring. All other items, stylists own.

Page 35 Dusty Blue

Bronte Velvet sofa, £900, Couch. Red Jielde lamp: find similar at Made in Design.

Page 70 Gunmetal

Parrot vase, £54, Rockett St George. Saarinen Table: find similar at Knoll.com. Swivel chair: find similar at Twenty Twenty One.

Page 43 Golden Yellow

Hand thrown vase, black, £59, white, £29 both Oggetto. Hand made Nest bowl, £22, French Connection Home. Bounce Chair, £295, Heal's. Mustard telephone, £49, Rockett St George. Sideboard: find similar at John Lewis. Lamp: find similar at Oka. Picture: find similar at Alfies Antique Market.

Page 39 Crimson

Blue mug, £20, Holly's House. Stone bottle, £5, Lost and Found. Glass bottle from a selection at Graham and Green. Wooden Table: find similar at Another Country. Wooden chair: find similar at Twenty Twenty One. Armchair: find similar at Heal's. Gubi Grasshoppa lamp: find similar at Skandium.

Page 40 Burgundy

Gold pendant light, £145, Rockett St George. Geometric vase, £42 for set 3, Rockett St George, painted in Citrine 71. Powder DLM Pink side table, painted in Light Peachblossom 3 £160, Holly's House.

Content Copyright © Belinda Corani, 2016

First published in 2016 by Home Conscious Ltd

Hollywood Court, Inglis Road, London W5 3RJ

The moral rights of Belinda Corani to be identified as the author of this written work have been asserted to by her in accordance with the Copyright, Design and Patents Act 1988

All rights reserved. No part of this publication may be reproduced, stored in a retrieval system or transmitted in any form by any means; electronic, electrostatic, magnetic tape, mechanical, photocopying, recording or otherwise without the permission of the Publisher.

ISBN – 978-0-9956921-0-7

Printed in Great Britain
by Amazon